TABLE OF CONTENTS

By studying this system for the bass guitar fretboard, you will learn a very organized and systematic method to understand the musical language on the bass guitar. By language, I am referring to the notes used to construct the scales and chords used to create a vocabulary that we each use to play music.

As bass players, it is often the case that we recognize harmony only if the root is at the beginning or bottom of the scale, chord or pattern we choose to play. Of course, in general, the role of the bass is to play chord roots and build grooves based on root movements combined with appropriate rhythms. While this is very important and a role we fully embrace, it is not enough. Embellishing or "decorating" grooves with added notes and playing fills will be enhanced by a more complete understanding of harmony and how it maps out on the neck. In addition, If and when you desire to play solos, this system will really help.

STUDY TIPS

Music is symmetrical. What happens in one key, happens identically in all keys.

The traditional bass guitar is also symmetrical (all strings tuned in the interval of perfect fourths). All scales, chords, patterns, positions will duplicate in each and every key with the same shape (no open strings) and patterns somewhere on the neck.

Music is a language of sound. I believe the ability to sing what you want to play is essential to speak the language authentically and create a vocabulary unique to you and your playing. Sing what you practice. Teach yourself the sounds of what you want to play.

Always play with a consistent time feel.

Memorize what you learn.

Now a couple of specific rules as you work through this material. Studying and performing are different. I have found that for studying, strict and clear rules will help you learn things effectively.

For this book, all material will be illustrated on a four-string bass. If you are using a bass with more strings, use the recommended guidelines and expand across the neck accordingly.

No open strings. All notes shall be fretted. This helps the symmetry and consistency of the patterns in all keys.

Scales (key centers) will be played starting with the lowest possible note on the neck regardless if it is the root of the scale.

All half step intervals will be played on the same string.

All exercises should be practiced in all five positions (and several keys).

These rules will become clear as you move through the material. If and when possible, it is highly recommended that you practice using some form of play-along app or device that provides a groove and chordal background. This will help you hear the sound of the key being practiced.

The spelling of the word "Music" would have no meaning if it were spelled "Usicm". Rearranging it does not create any word or idea that we recognize or use in English. In music however, rearranging and re-spelling scales and chords creates very valuable and common vocabulary. C major is spelled CDEFGAB. In changing the starting note to "D" and respelling the scale DEFGABC we have something of value commonly used for vocabulary in music. In fact, the new spelling creates a minor scale. It is referred to as a mode of the major key.

In a sense both spellings, starting from "C" and starting from "D", create lines:

CDEFGAB

DEFGABC

Each has a very defined starting and end point. While very important, this is a short and somewhat limited fingering pattern. By creating a **circle of the key of "C"** and all keys, any of the notes can be designated as the beginning (root). This approach will help in understanding how harmony is on the neck in **five specific positions,** covering the entire neck with one vocabulary (key).

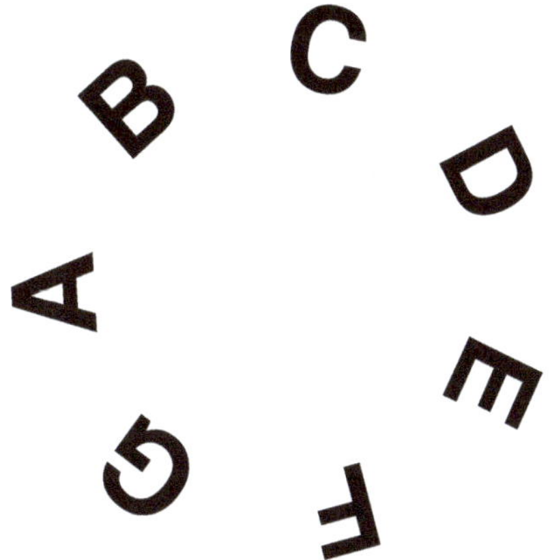

For the first examples, every position is a circle of the key that has a "C" root, even when "C" is not the lowest note of the shape. (The positions are not to be confused with the seven modes spelling of a key, although the positions apply to the modes as well).

Now let's look at the five positions of the key of "C" major. The lowest note creating a position that does not require open strings is "G" at the third fret of the E string. The high note in this position is "C" at the fifth fret of the G string.

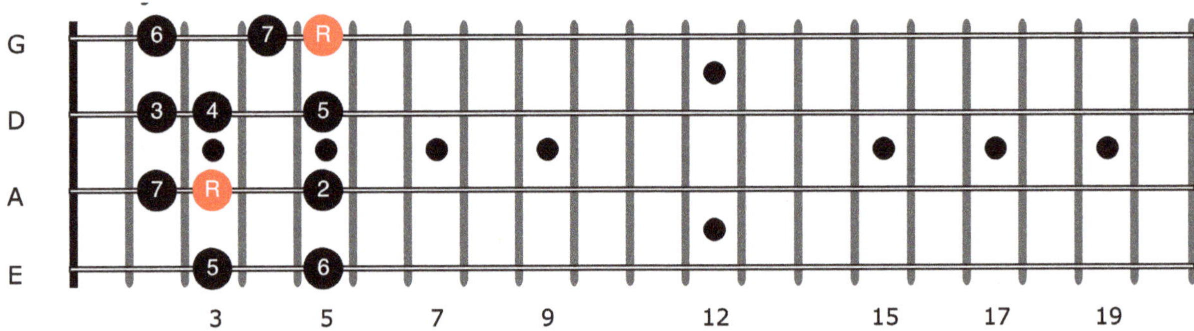

As we shift and rotate the circle of this key up the neck, the next starting note is "A". It is the note following "G" and will create a position that ends with "D" on the G string at the seventh fret.

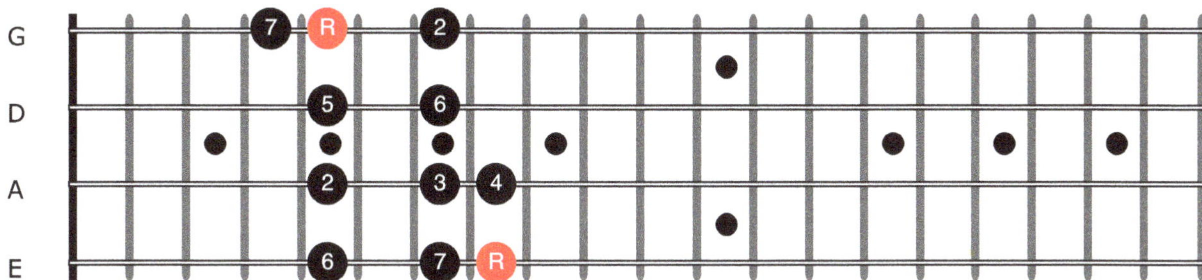

The next starting note is "B/C". The top note is "F".

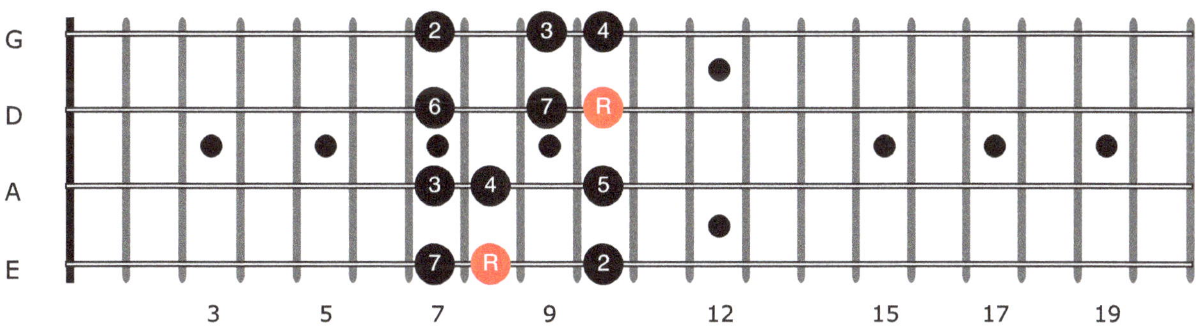

Due to the fact that "C" is only a half-step above "B", there is not a new position generated. It is this fact of two half steps in a major key (between 3-4 and 7-R) that illuminates why there are only five positions for a seven-note key (scale). Remember this is not to be confused with the seven "modes" of a key.

Next is "D" at the tenth fret of the E string is the low note of the next position. Top note is "G" on the G string.

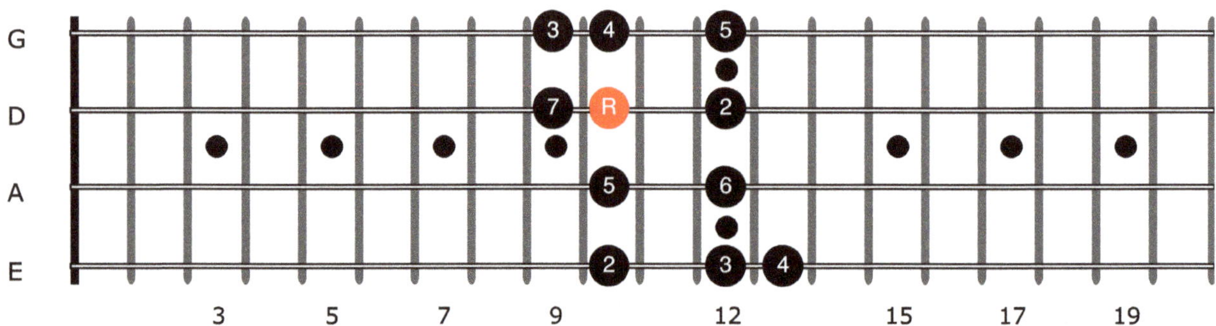

The last position begins with "E/F" (*"F" is a half-step away and does not create a new position*). "A" at the twelfth fret is the top note of this shape.

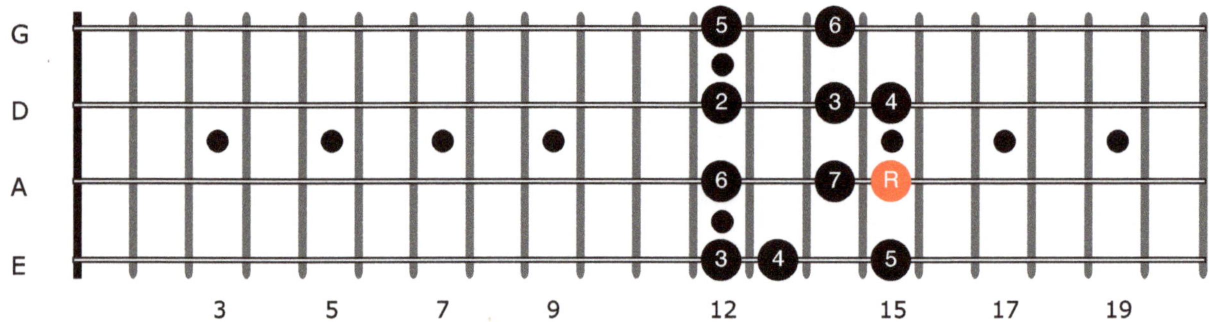

Play up and down each position repeatedly to begin the process of familiarity with the fingerings and shapes. Remember, all the notes are in the key of "C".

It is these five circles (shapes and positions) that outline this key. Because of the symmetry of music and the bass, all keys will be duplicated. **Five identical shapes for all keys!**

Before we begin a series of exercise drills involving **sequences, intervals and chord arpeggios** in these positions, look at the key of "G". A comparison with the key of "C" will illustrate the same five position shapes that we learned in that key.

Play through all the positions of the key of "G".

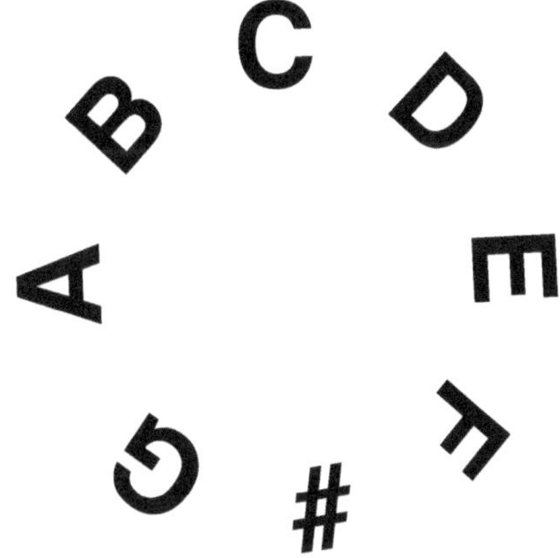

In this key, try ascending one position, shifting to the next position, and then descend back down it. Practice this "*one up, one down*" drill through all five positions.

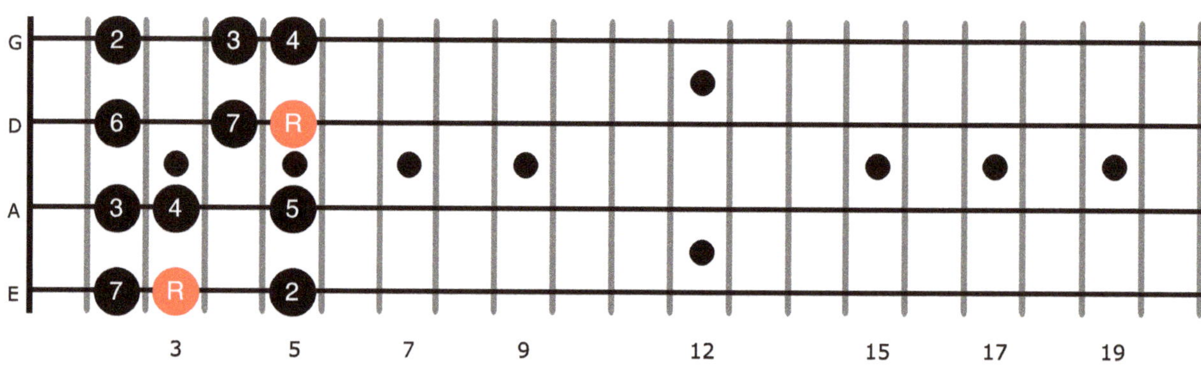

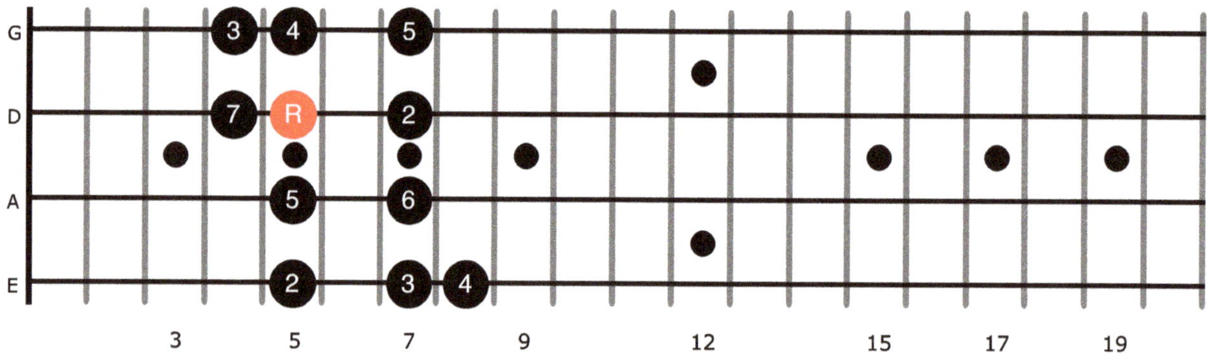

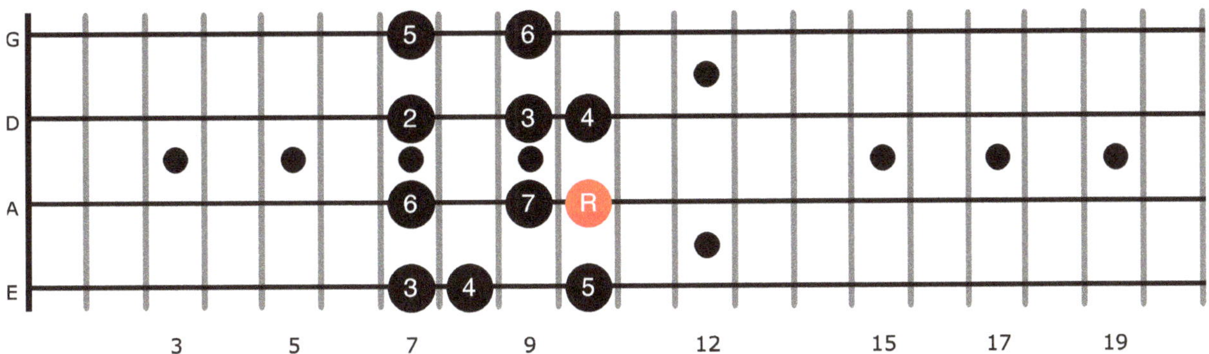

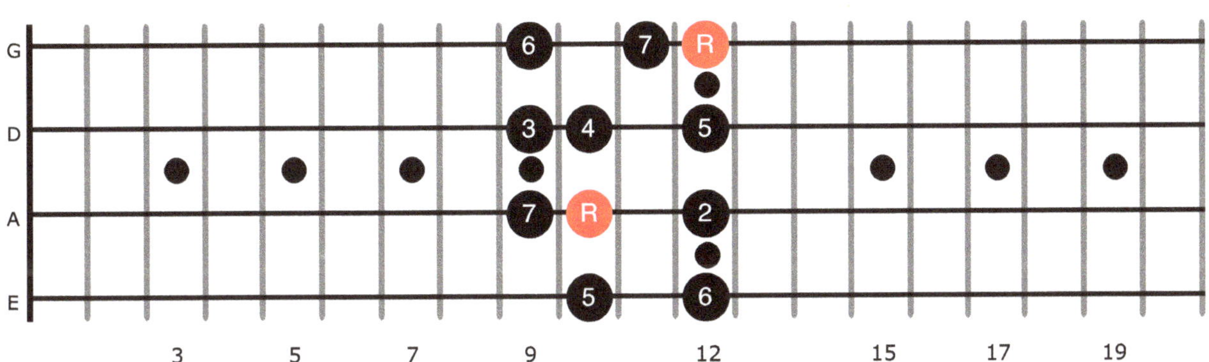

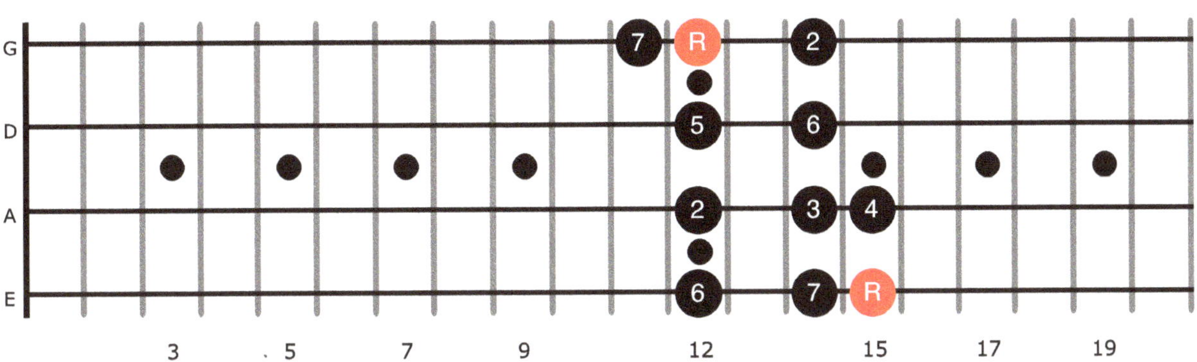

The first exercise is a four-note ascending sequence that will repeat starting from each note of the key available in a single position. Start with the lowest note of the pattern and play up four notes.

Practicing in the key of "F", the low note of the bottom position is "G" on the E string. The last sequence possible in this position will start at "G" on the D string. As you descend back down the neck, play the same ascending direction of the four-note sequence. This position does have a one fret shift that occurs that adds to the challenge of the sequence exercise.

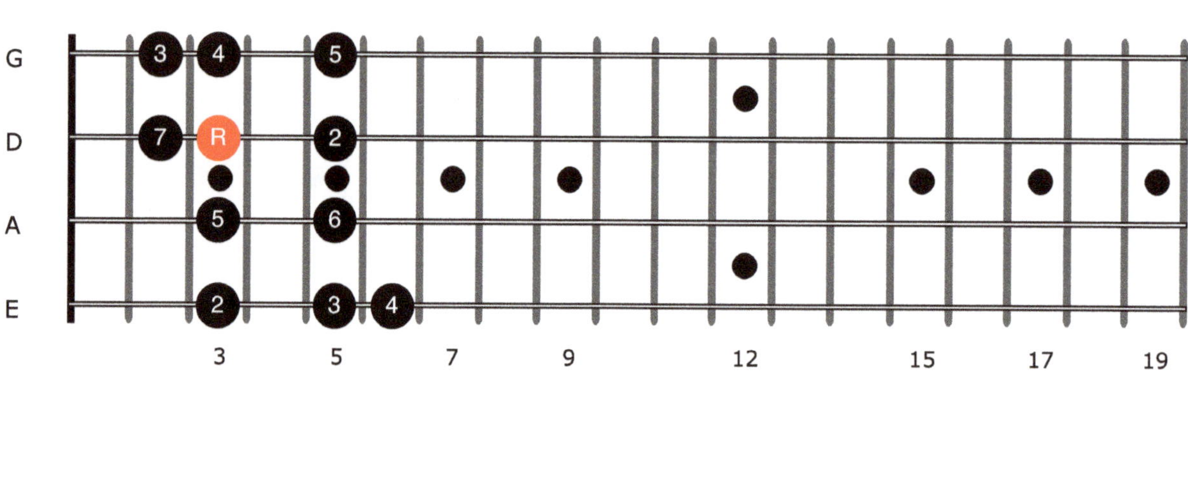

Moving to the next position, repeat the four-note sequence starting at "A" at the fifth fret of the E string. The last available sequence in this position starts at "A" on the D string.

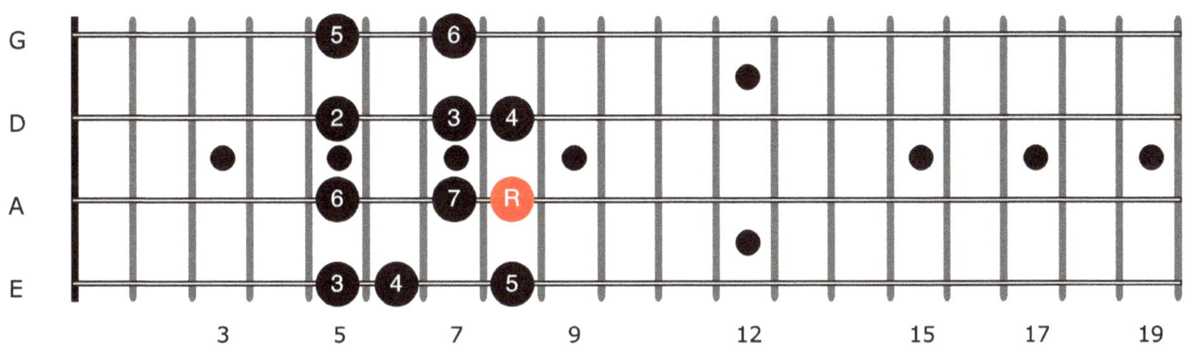

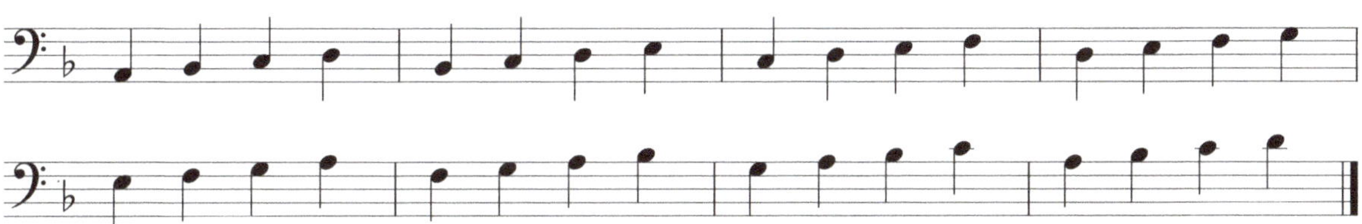

Continue this sequence drill in each of the remaining positions of the key of "F".

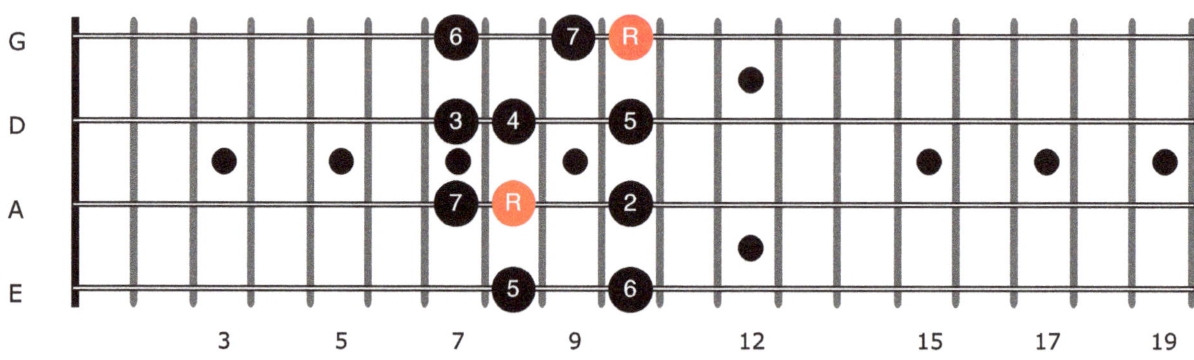

Now from the position starting on "D" at the tenth fret.

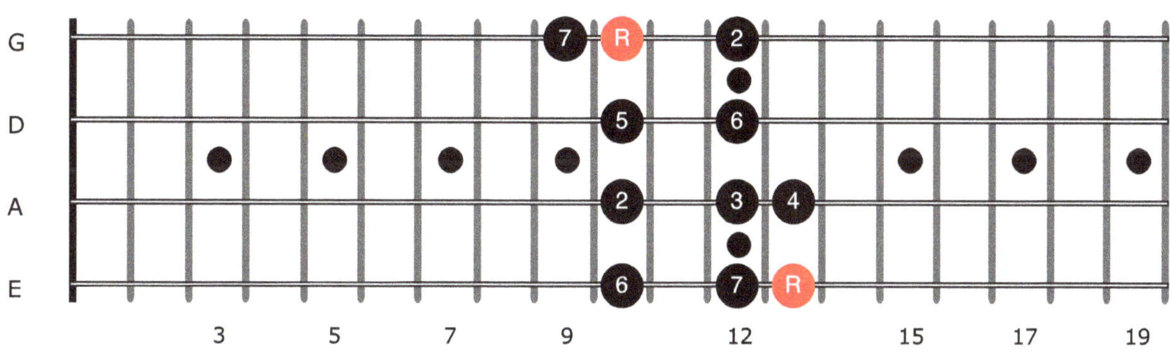

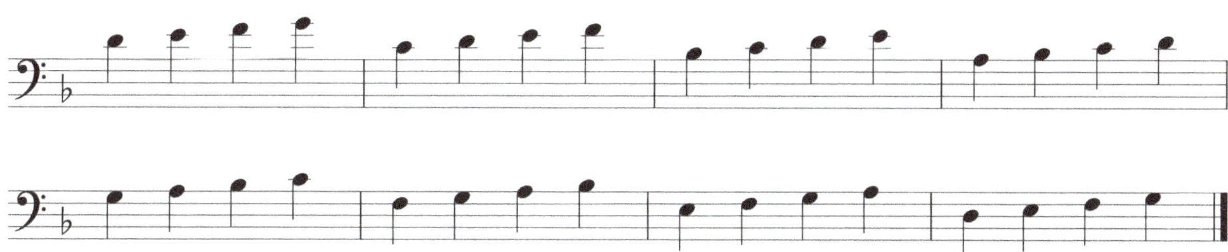

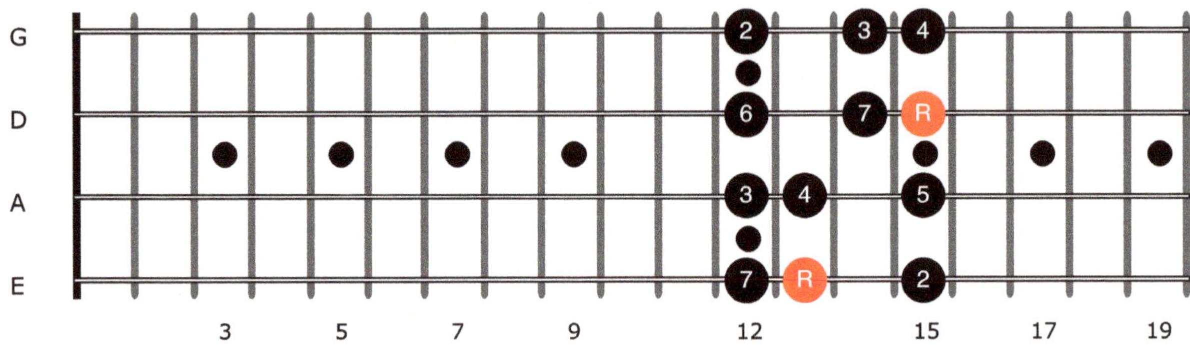

For this drill use the diatonic 4-note sequence to play up and down *(horizontal)* the neck as opposed to across (*vertical*) the neck in a single position. By playing each sequence on two strings only, it requires a shift from one position to the next to complete all of the sequences. The five positions still guide us for where to play the notes from the key (F major). Notice that as a result of the half step intervals in the key (between 3-4 and 7-R) there are still just five positions used for all seven notes of the key. **For this approach, when the next starting note is a whole step away, shift to a new position. Starting notes a half-step apart will be played in the same position.**

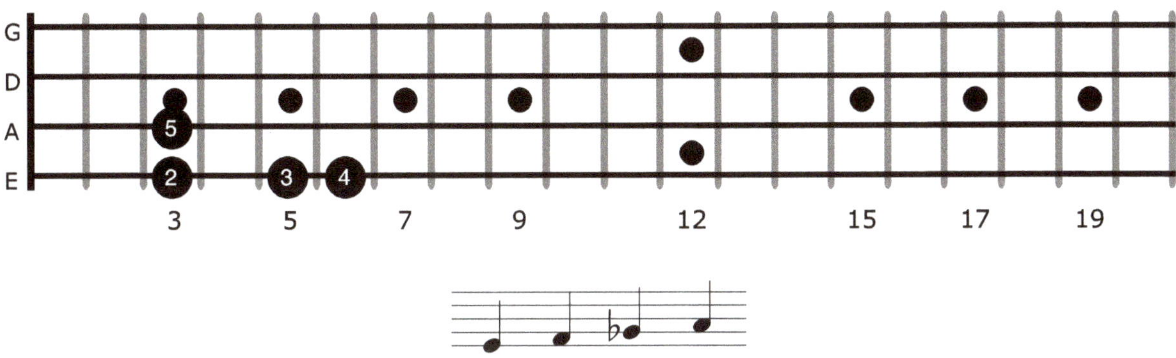

The next starting note for the sequence is "A" which is a whole step away from "G" and is played in the next position. Following "A" is "Bb" and due to the half step interval between them, is played in the same position as "A".

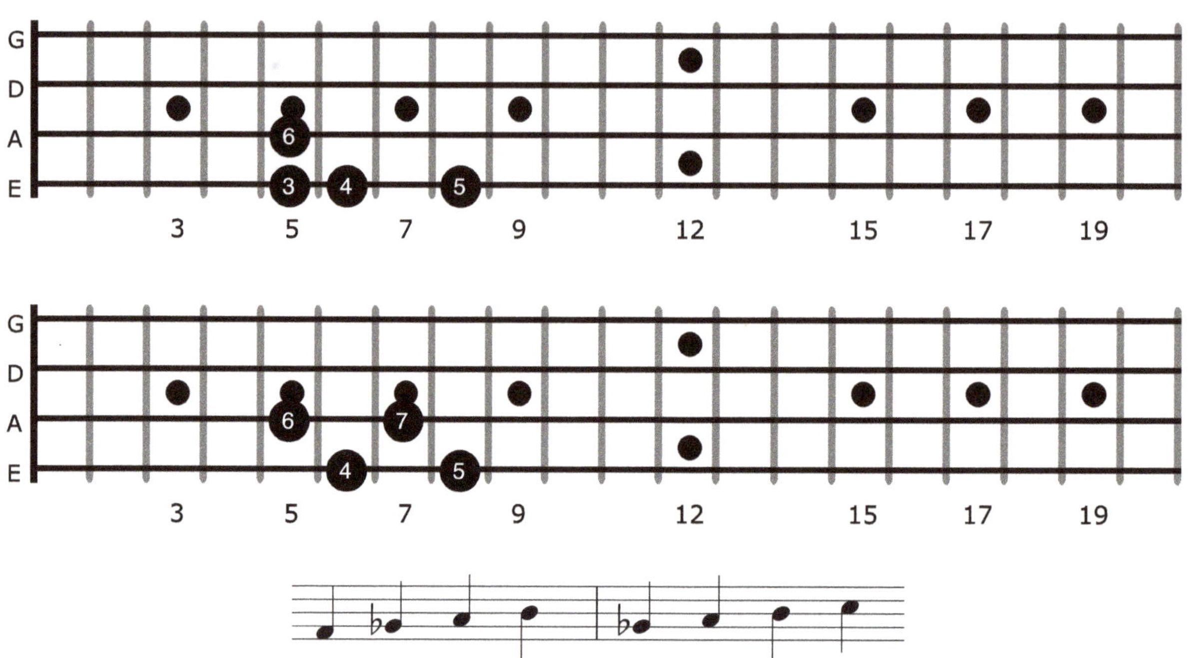

A whole step from "Bb" is "C" at the eighth fret.

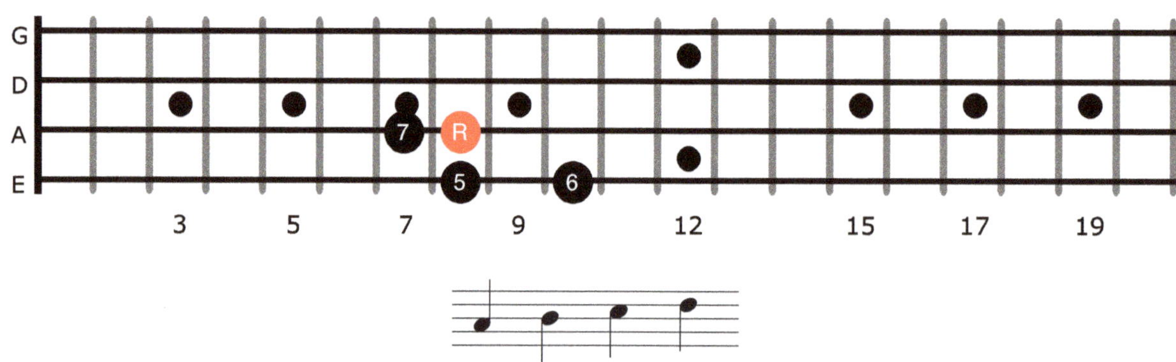

"D" is a whole step away and begins in the next position.

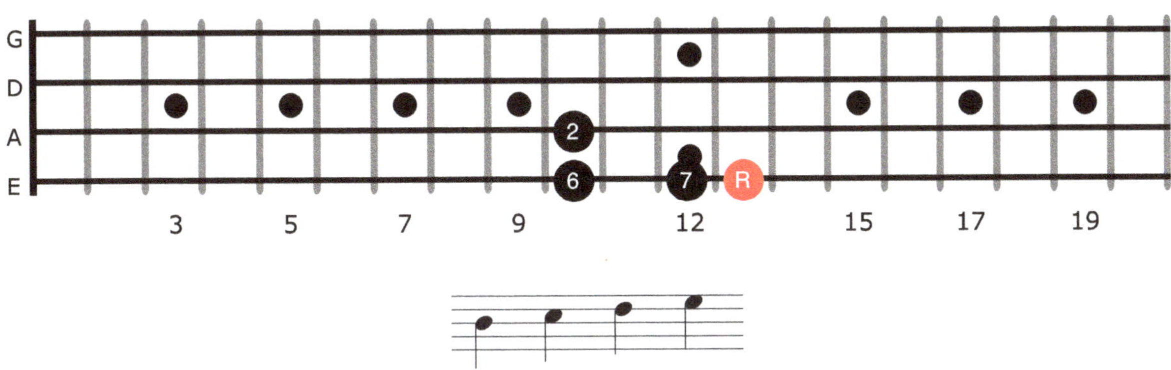

Sequences from "E" and "F" will be played in the position at the twelfth fret.

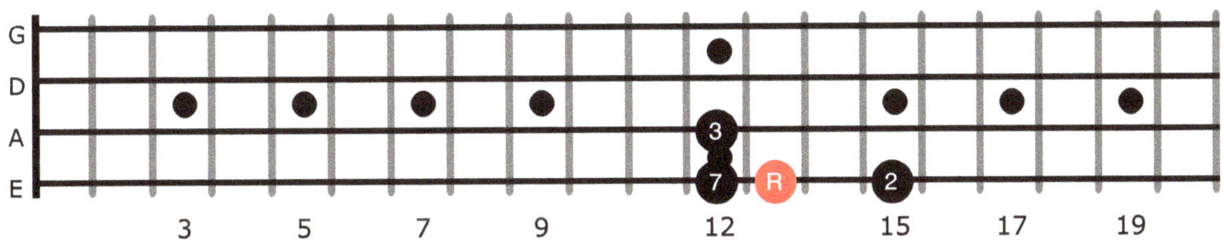

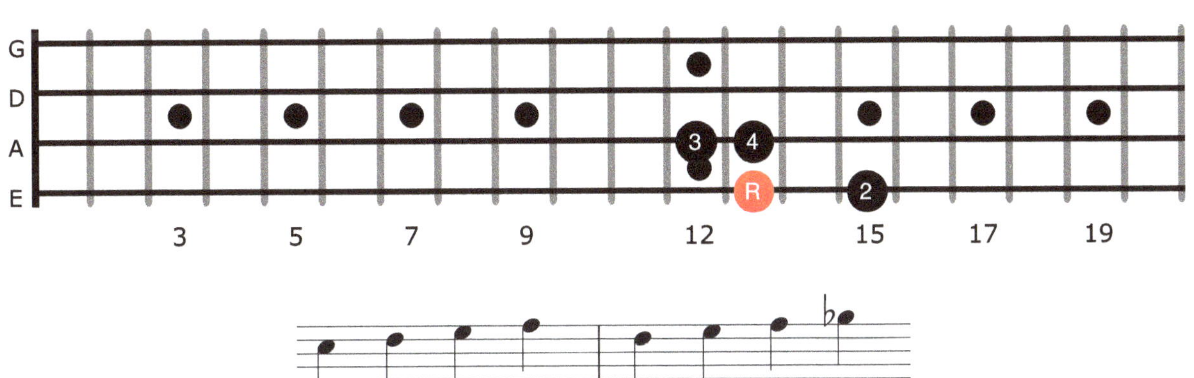

Now play a continuous sequence from one position to the next without stopping. This is a great way to become adept at moving key center vocabulary up and down the neck in a logical and organized way. New groove and fill ideas will result in this expanded understanding. Start slow but increase the speed as you get more comfortable.

Descend the neck with the same sequence.

Next step is to move the four-note "F" major sequence to the A and D strings. The same guidelines of position shifting apply.

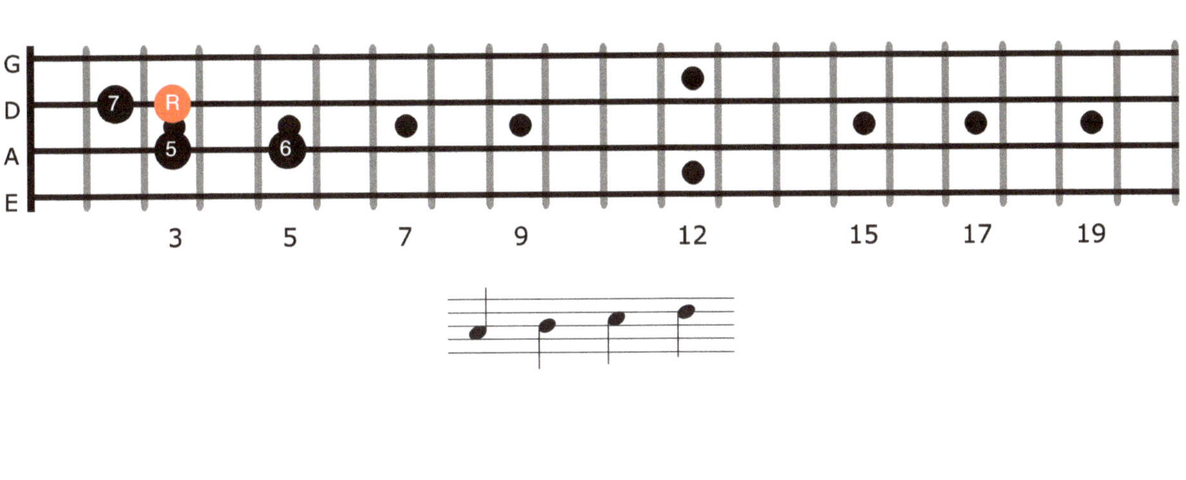

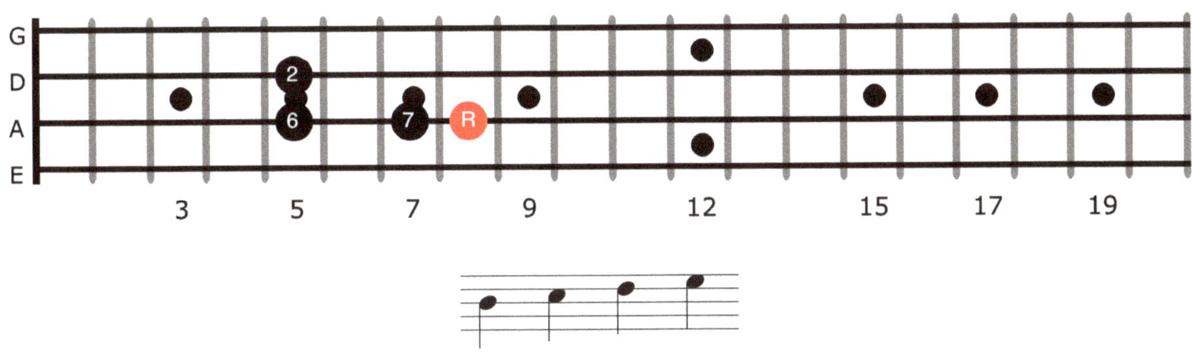

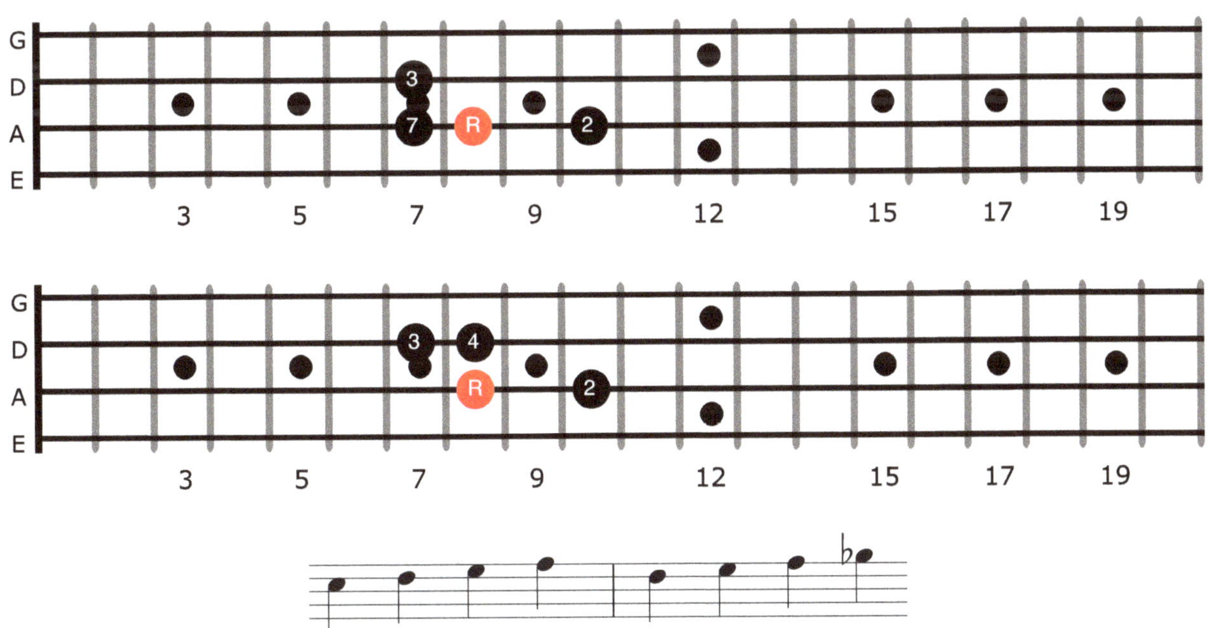

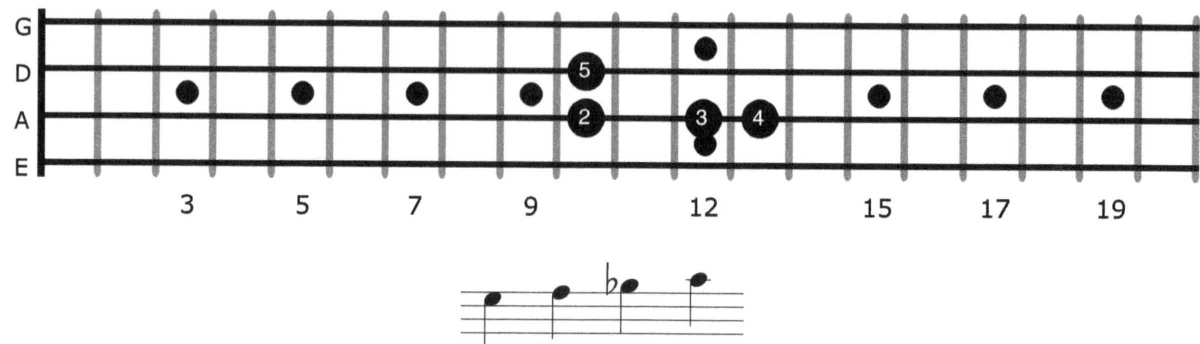

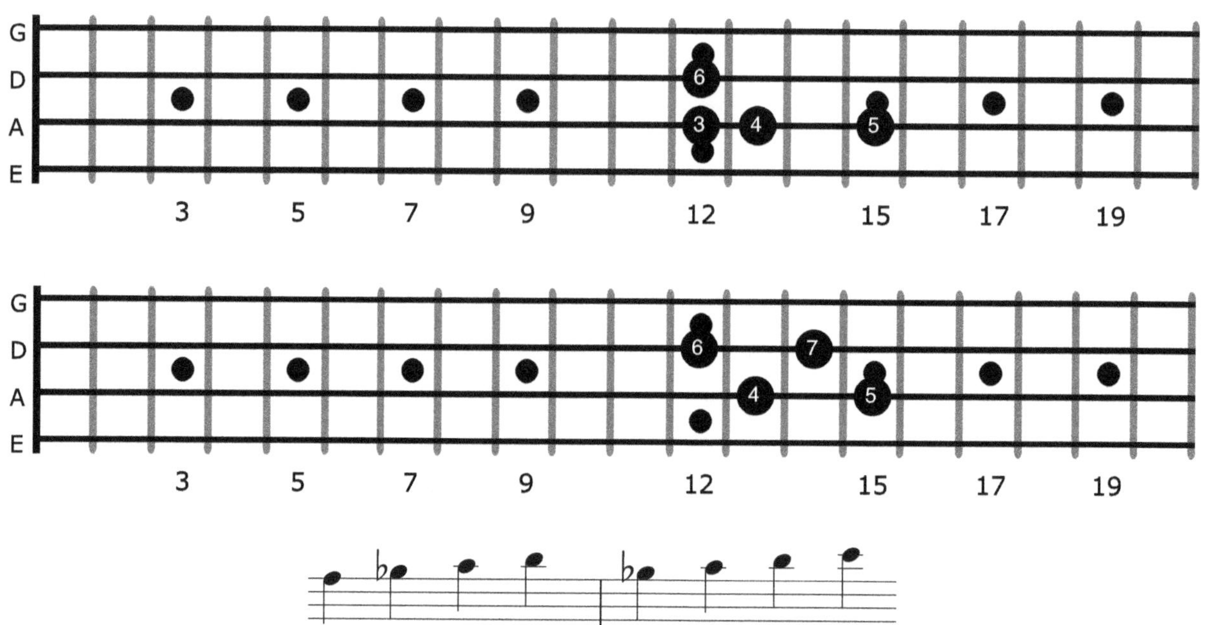

Now play a continuous sequence from one position to the next without stopping. Also descend the neck with the same sequences.

Finally, play the same sequence in the key of "F" on the D and G strings.

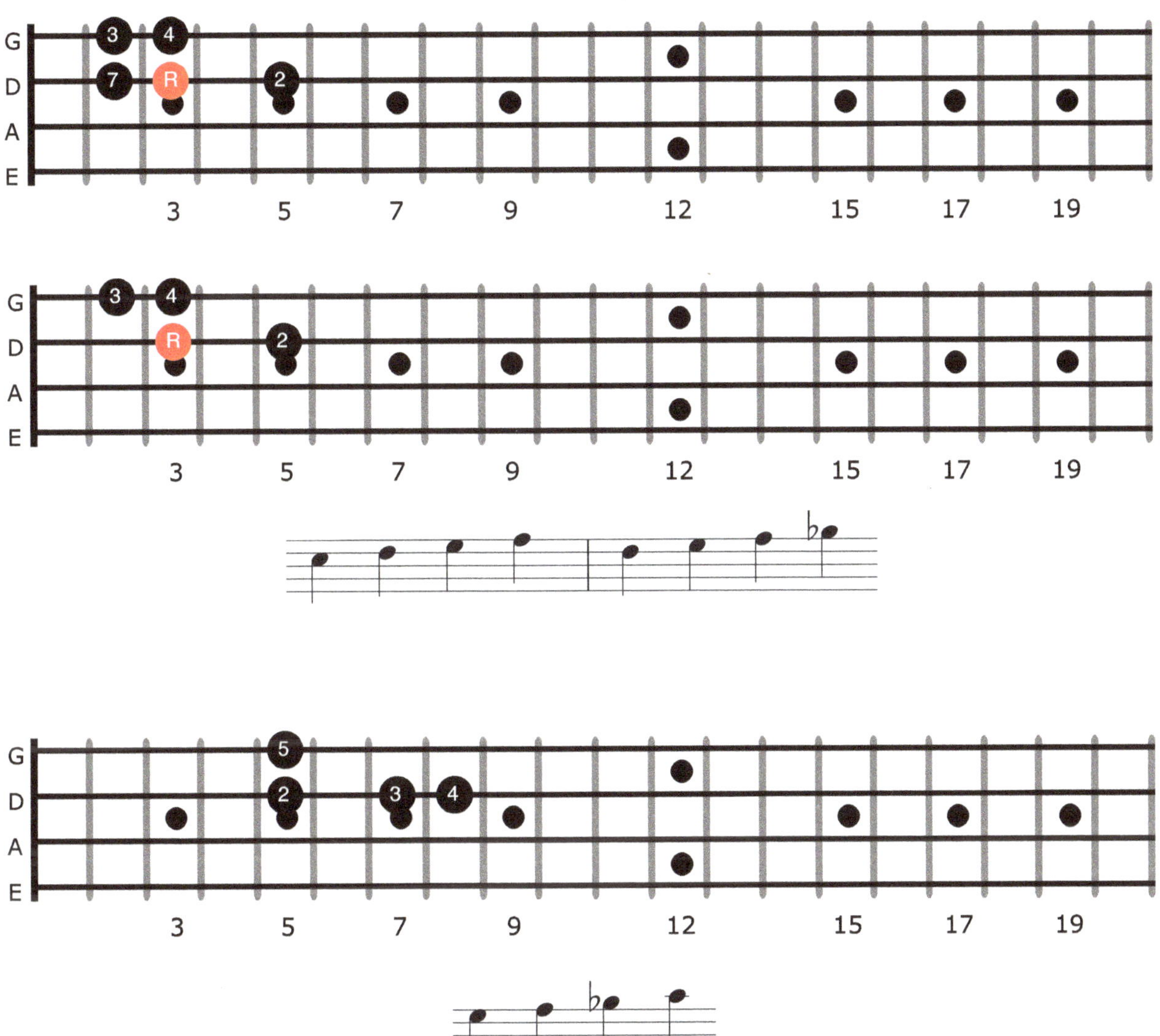

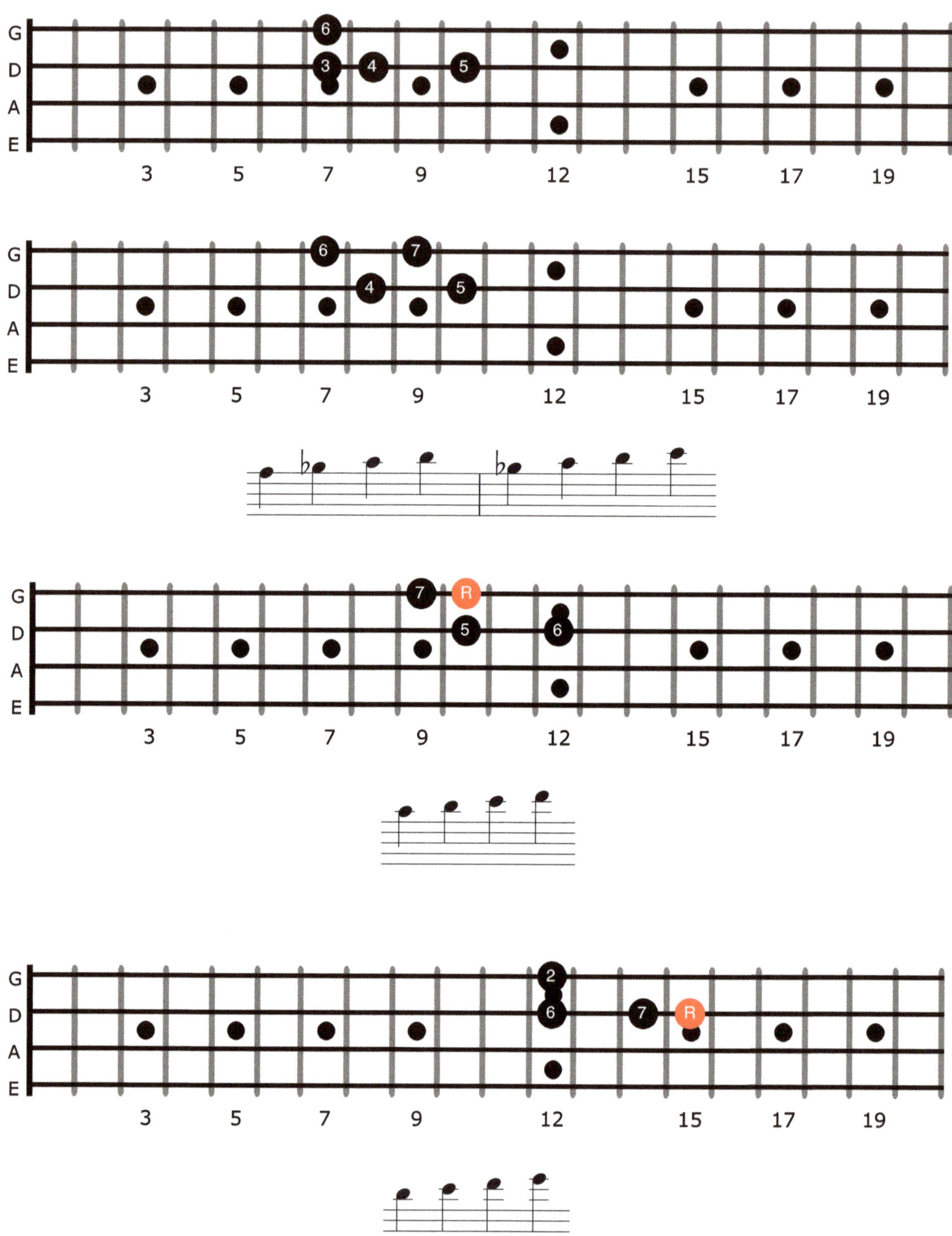

Now play a continuous sequence from one position to the next without stopping. Also descend the neck with the same sequences.

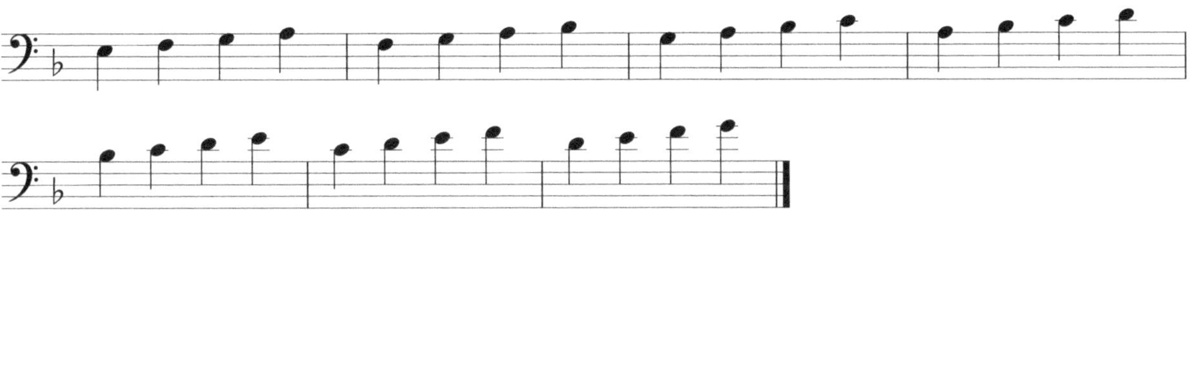

Two approaches have been introduced using the positions. First is a "**vertical**" approach, playing across all strings in a single position. The second is a "**horizontal**" approach using two strings only and playing up and down the neck using the positions as a guide. Both are important and are necessary to be fully adept at navigating the bass neck.

Here are a couple of examples of using this type of sequence as a fill during a bass groove.

PRACTICE GROOVES

One option for where to play this example would be at the very bottom of the bass using the open A and D strings. In fact, this may be the first choice.

Try playing it in the bottom position of "F" major (no open strings).

Equally important is to practice it using the two-string approach shifting through multiple positions.

As is evident by now, there are several locations on the bass neck to pay most notes. Deciding where on the neck to play lines is a big part of the challenge to the bass guitar.

The range of this example is fairly large, "F" at the first fret and an "F" two octaves higher.

The fill could be played in either the fourth (low note of the position would be "D" on the E string) or the fifth position (12th fret). However, returning to the low "F" becomes an important consideration.

Practice a two-string *"**horizontal**"* (shifting down through multiple positions) approach on the D and G strings. This will put you back at the bottom of the bass preparing you to play the low "F".

This first interval exercise will be ascending, **diatonic thirds** in each of the five positions. All notes should be played only where they are located in the position shapes. Continue ascending (root first and then third) the interval of thirds even when descending back down the position from high to low. Variations of this will be introduced later.

Examples for this exercise are in the key of "D". Start the interval drill on "F#" (being that it is the lowest available diatonic note in the bottom position). Continue through the shape until you reach the final available diatonic root-third interval which in this key is from "G" to "B".

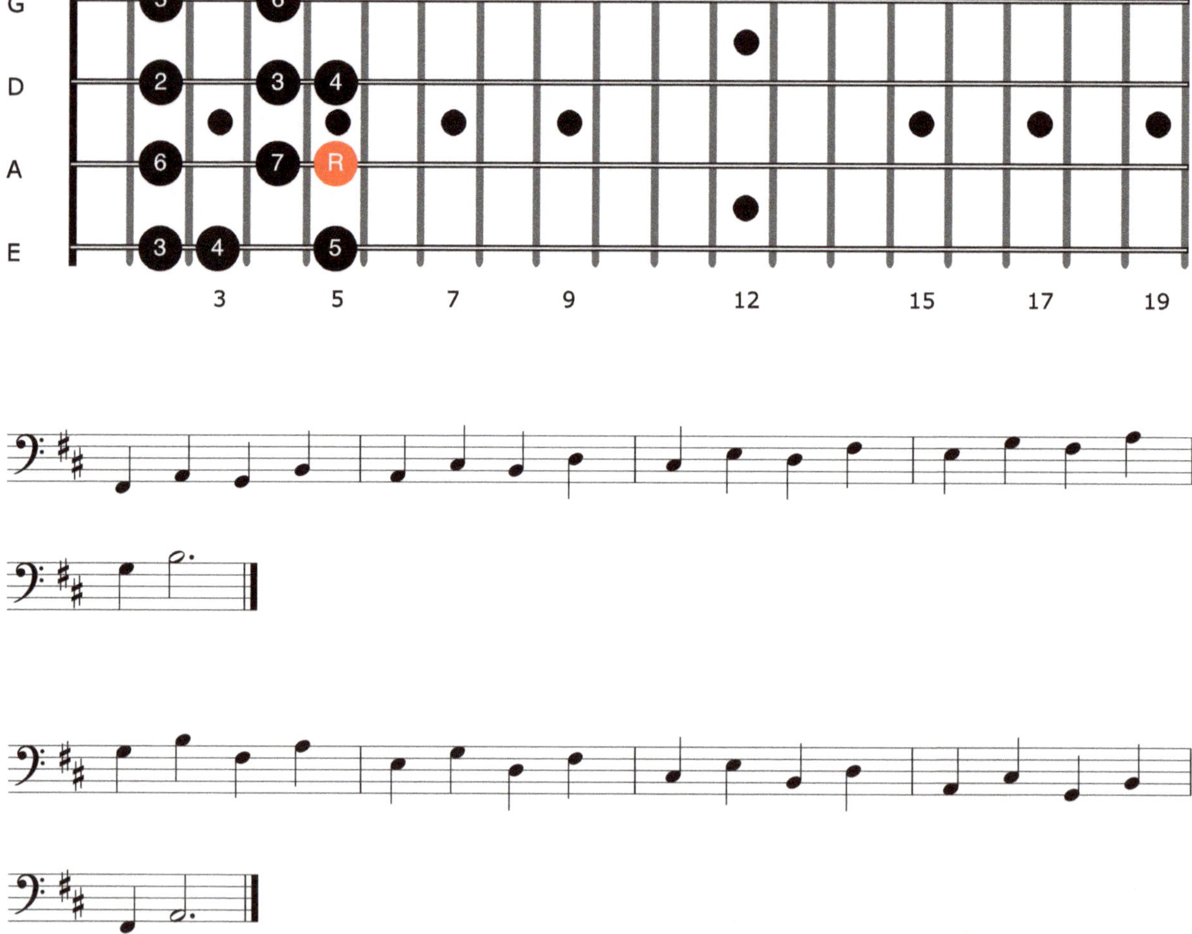

This position starts on "A" at the fifth fret. Continue the diatonic thirds in the key of "D". The last available third in this position is "B" to "D".

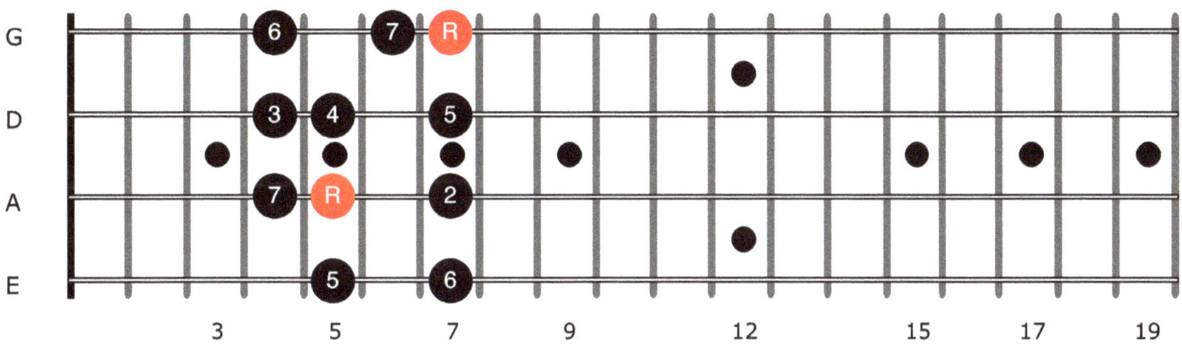

Next the position located at the seventh fret.

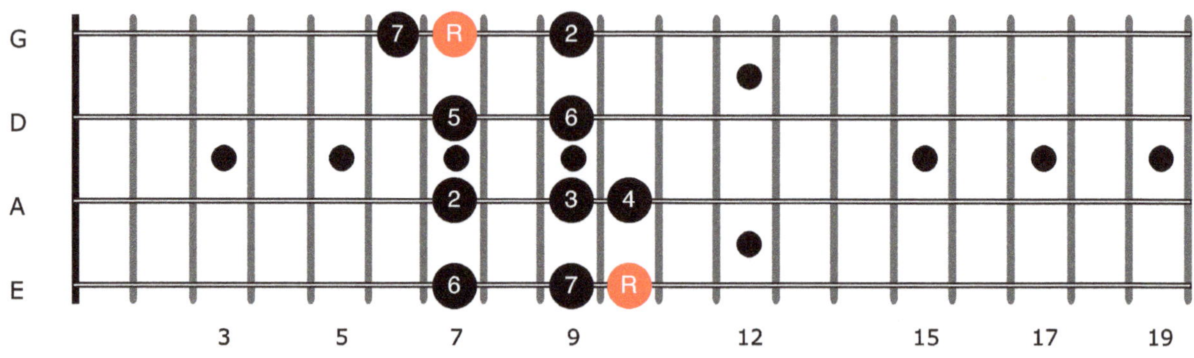

Continue with the position of "C#/D" at the ninth fret.

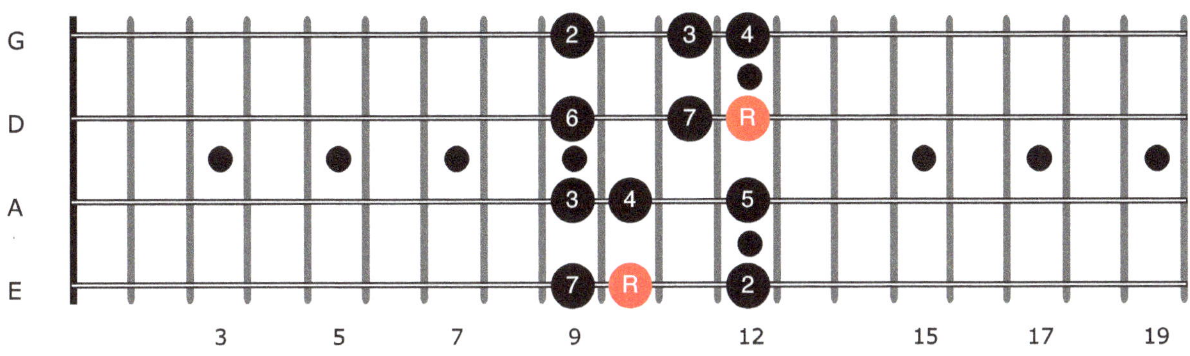

Finish this ascending, diatonic thirds exercise in the last position at the twelfth fret.

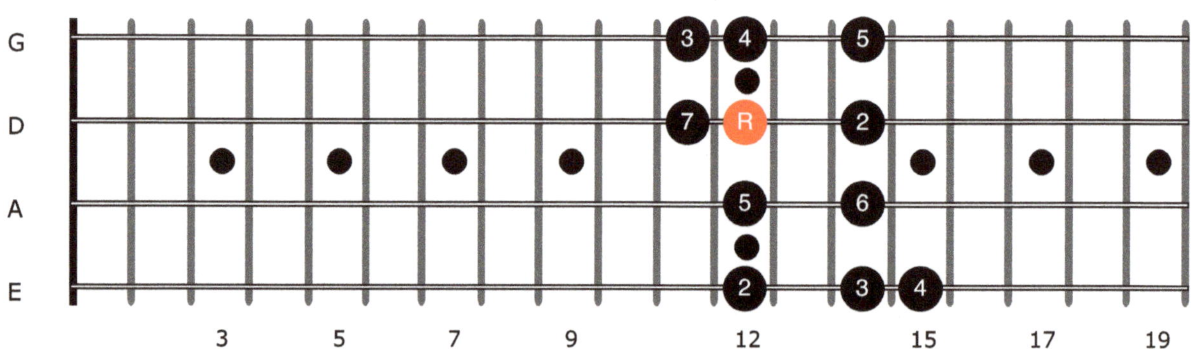

Like the sequence drill, the next step is a two-string approach played up and down the neck ("*horizontal*") shifting through the five positions. The interval is still diatonic thirds in the key of "D". The direction of the interval will continue to be ascending even when descending the neck.

This horizontal approach is a challenge and helps to facilitate a complete control of the neck.

A couple of details about this exercise that you should observe and to which you should adhere.

There is one shape for a minor third (both notes are played on the same string), and one shape for a major third (two strings). **This does not mean however that there is only one shape for major and minor thirds.

Due to the half steps in a major key (3-4 and 7-R) two positions have two sets of thirds.

Shift to the next position when the next starting note is a whole step away.

The quality (major or minor) of the third corresponds to the quality of the chord created on the same note. For example, the first third in the bottom position is "F#" to "A". That is a minor third. The chord in D major built on "F#" is F#mi.

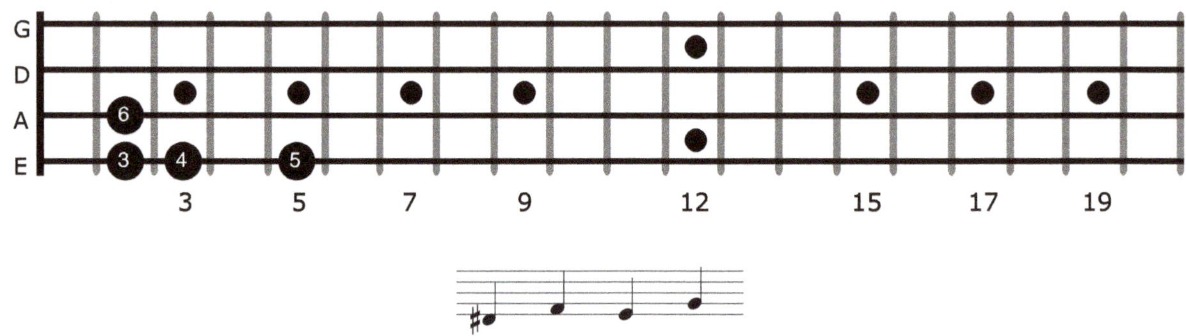

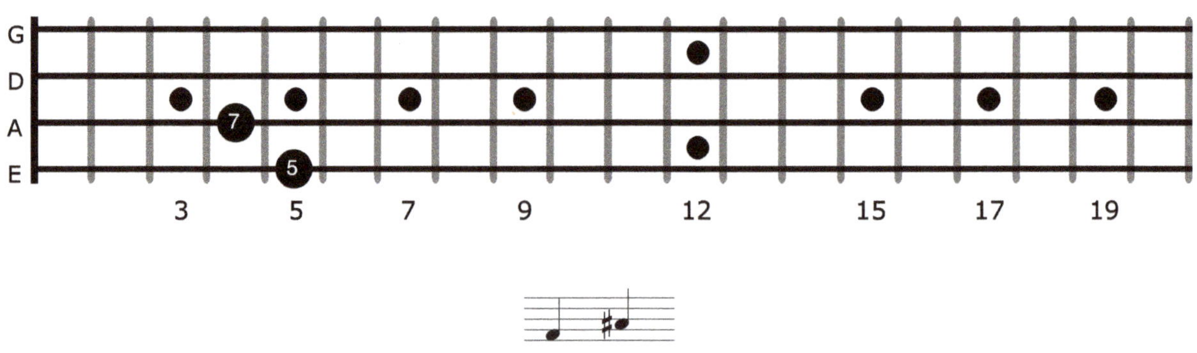

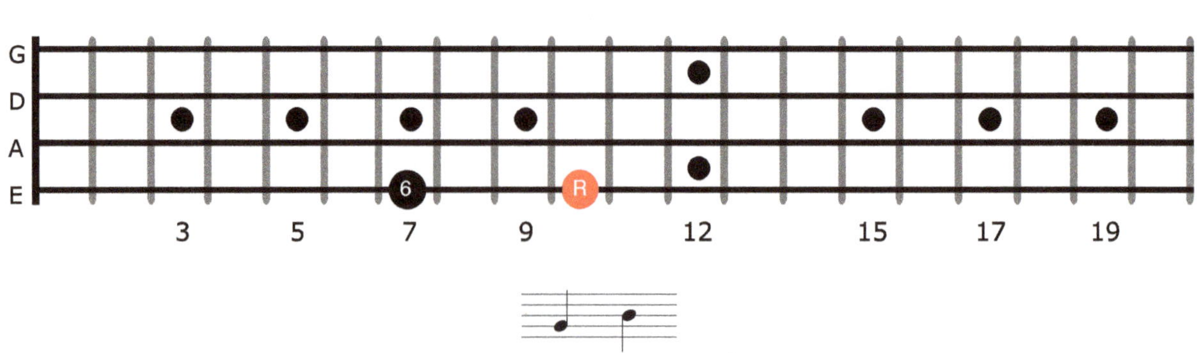

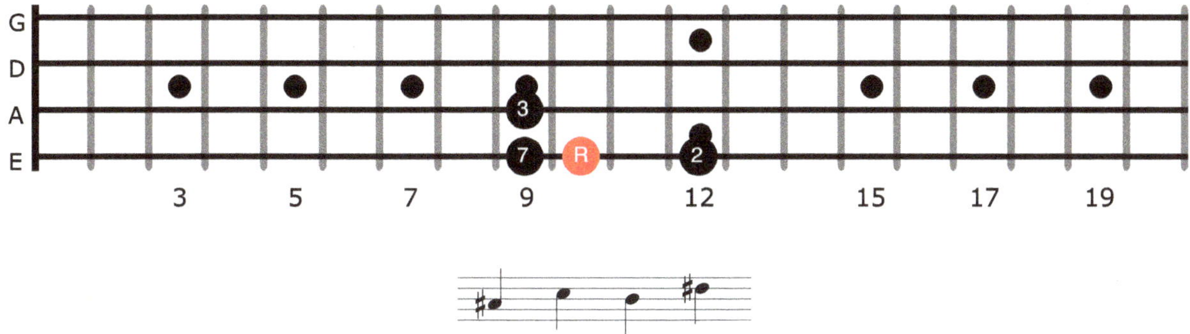

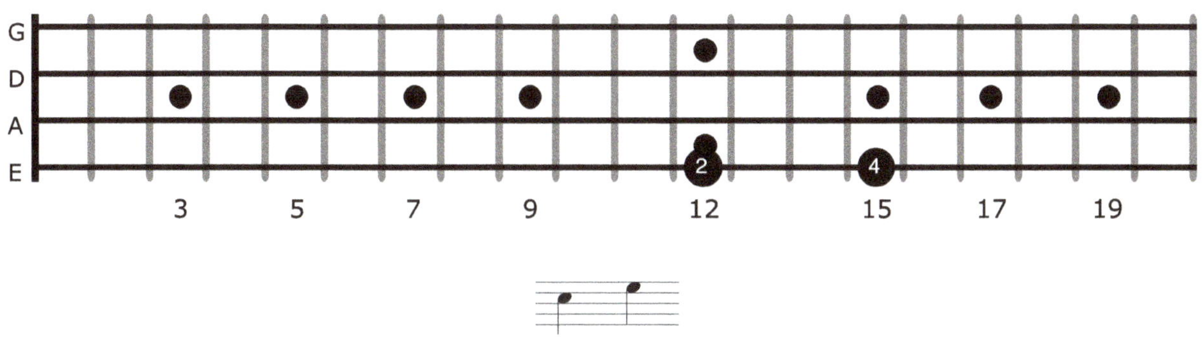

Play the two-string interval drill shifting up and down the neck between positions without stopping. Keep the direction, low note (root) to high note (3rd), of the interval consistent even when descending the neck. Notice that for this example, there is a resolution to the root ("D") of the key after ascending and descending the neck.

Play this on the E string and A string only

All minor thirds on the E and all major thirds on the E and A strings. This will ensure proper shifting through all five positions.

The "D" (root of the key) on beat 4 of the second measure should be played on the E string.

The "D" (root of the key) on beat 4 of the fourth measure should be played on the A string.

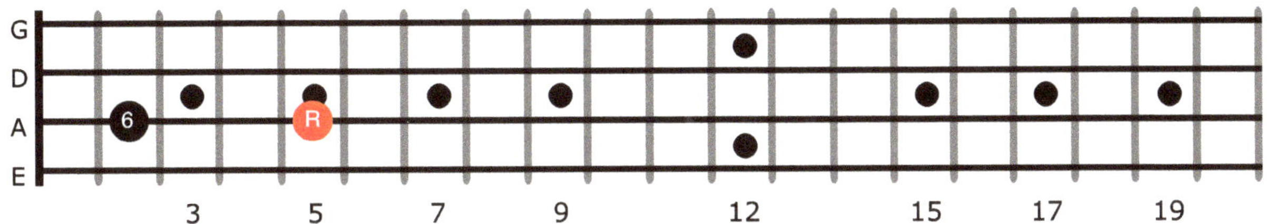

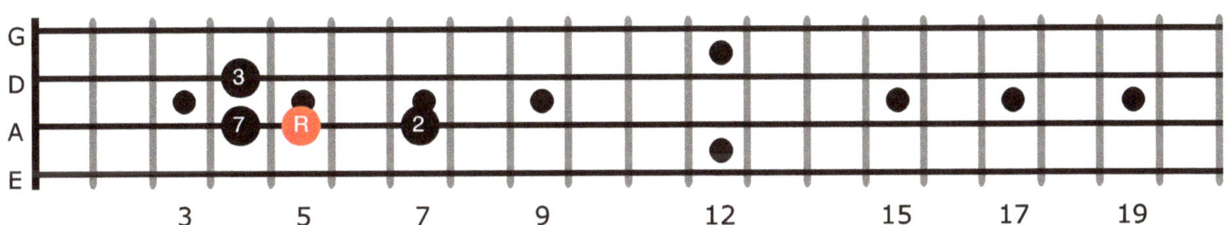

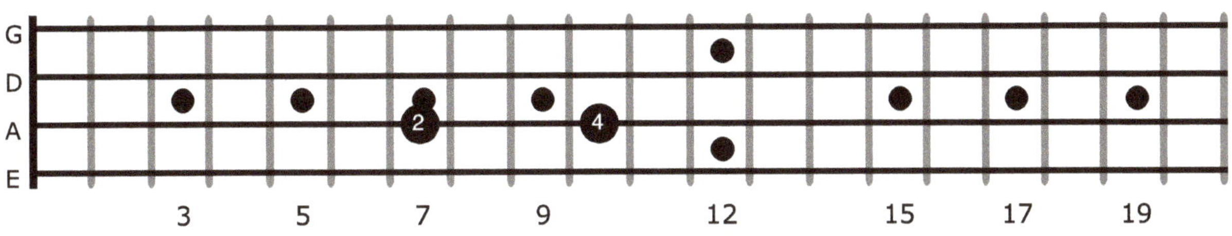

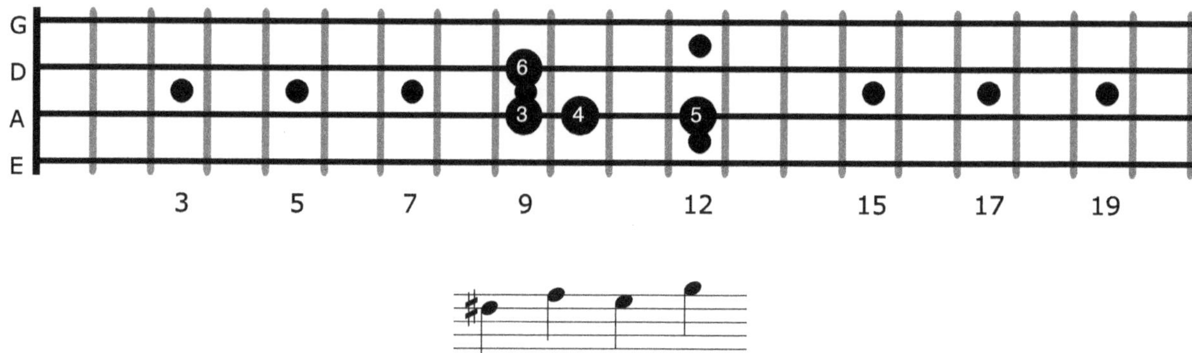

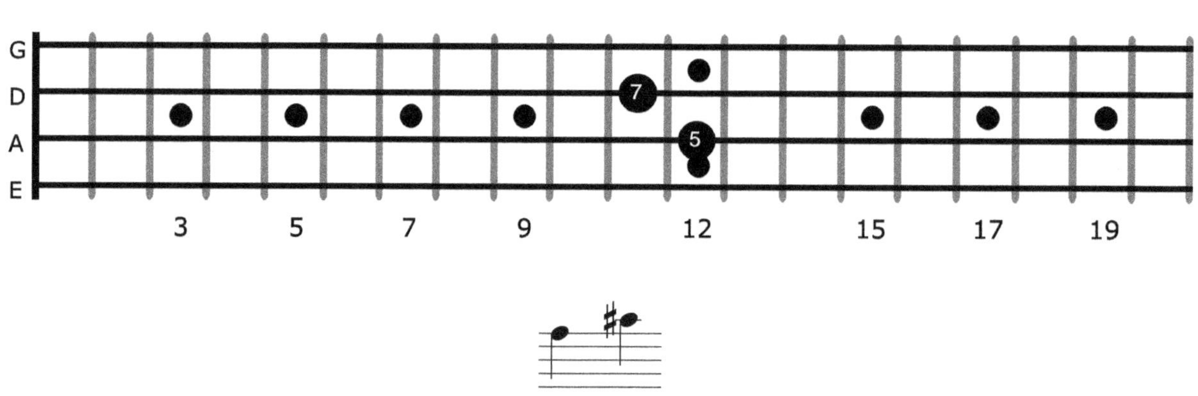

Next play the two-string interval drill shifting up and down the neck between positions without stopping. Keep the direction, low note (root) to high note (3rd), of the interval consistent even when descending the neck.

Play this on the A string and D string only

All minor thirds on the A string and all major thirds on the A and D strings. This will ensure proper shifting through all five positions.

The "D" (root of the key) on beat 4 of the second measure should be played on the D string (twelfth fret).

The "D" (root of the key) on beat 4 of the fourth measure should be played on the A string.

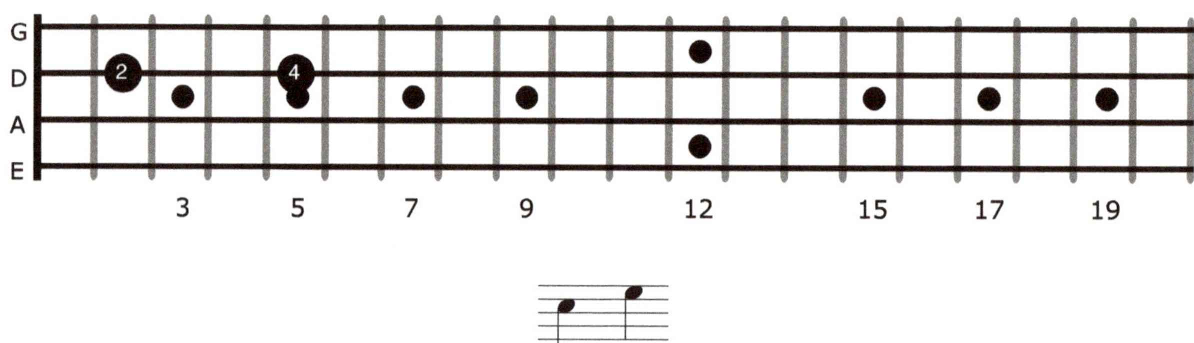

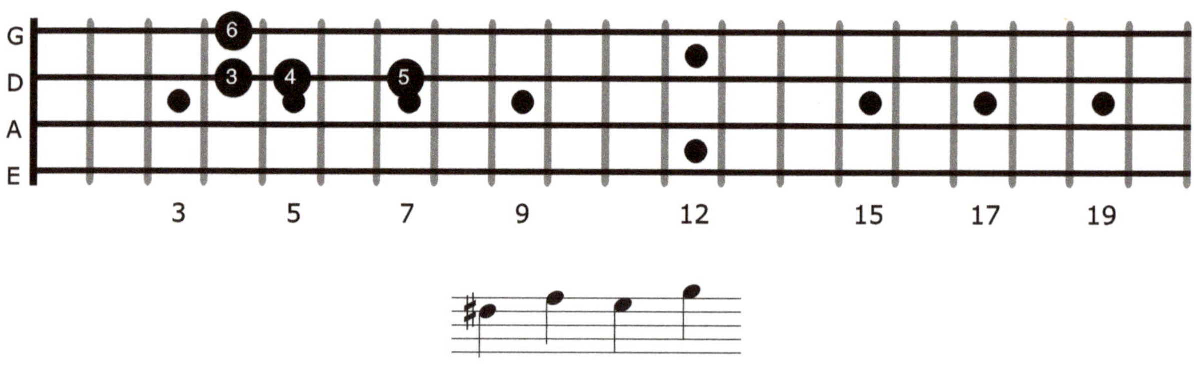

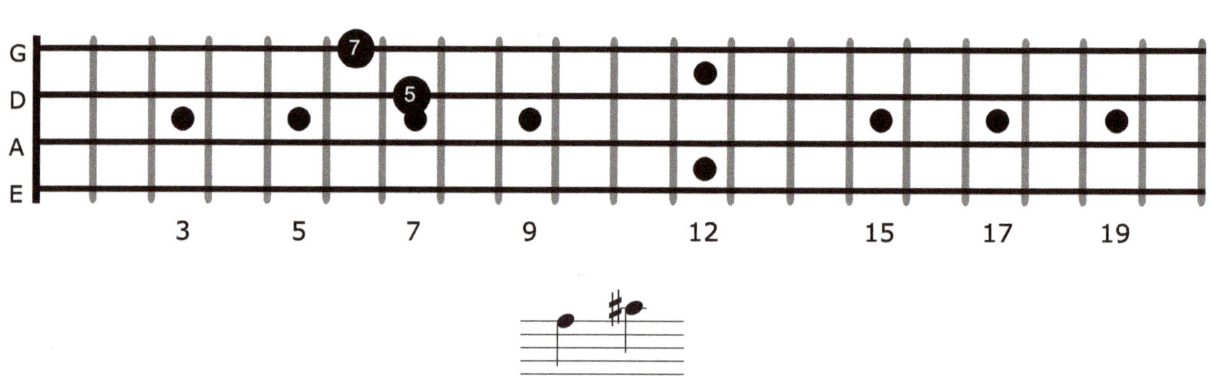

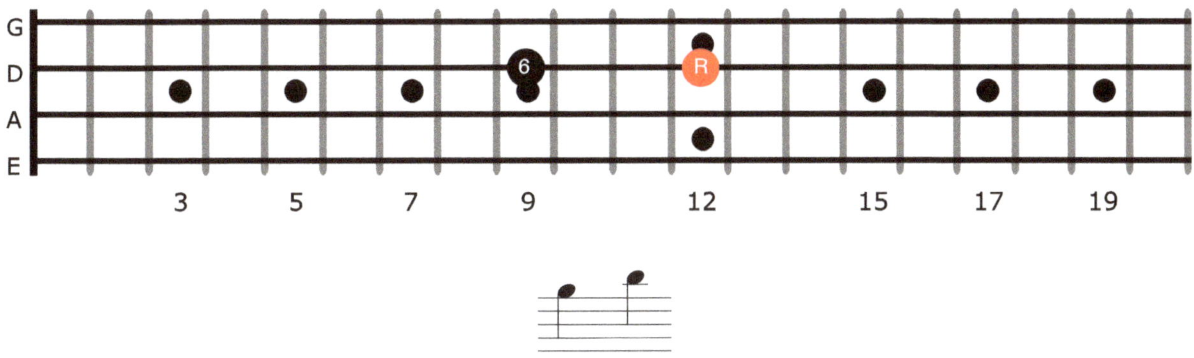

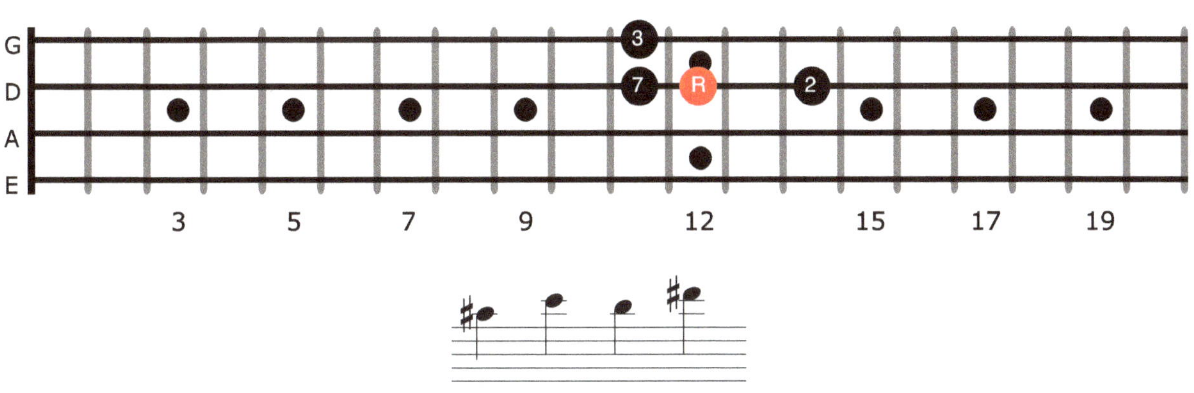

Next play the two-string interval drill shifting up and down the neck between positions without stopping. Keep the direction, low note (root) to high note (3rd), of the interval consistent even when descending the neck.

Play this on the D string and G string only.

All minor thirds on the D and all major thirds on the D and G strings. This will ensure proper shifting through all five positions.

The "D" (root of the key) on beat 4 of the second measure should be played on the D string (twelfth fret).

The "D" (root of the key) on beat 4 of the fourth measure should be played on the A string at the fifth fret.

Here are a couple of examples of bass lines using "D" major diatonic thirds.

To adhere to the practice guidelines, play this example with no open strings in the bottom position of "D" major.

Play the first two measures of this example at the "C#/D" position at the ninth fret.

Measure three is a transition bar where a shift to the bottom of the neck is necessary.

Play the last measure in an "horizontal approach" (E and A strings). To adhere to the drill guidelines, play the major thirds ("G" to "B" and "A" to "C#") on two strings and the minor thirds ("B" to "D" and "C#" to "E") on one string. This approach will organize a shift back up the neck to the "D" at the tenth fret.

This next series of drills is constructed from the diatonic triads from the key of "Bb" major. The triads are: Bbma, Cmi, Dmi, Ebma, Fma, Gmi and Adim.

The first set of exercises are the "*vertical*" approach. All of the available triads will be played in a single position. This will be done in each of the five positions. All arpeggios will be constructed in root position.

Remember that music is symmetrical and the order of chord quality (ie: major, minor or diminished) is the same in all keys.

In the first position, the lowest available triad is "Gmi" which is the VI chord of this key. The sequence of each triad is root, third and fifth. Play this sequence even as you descend back down the position.

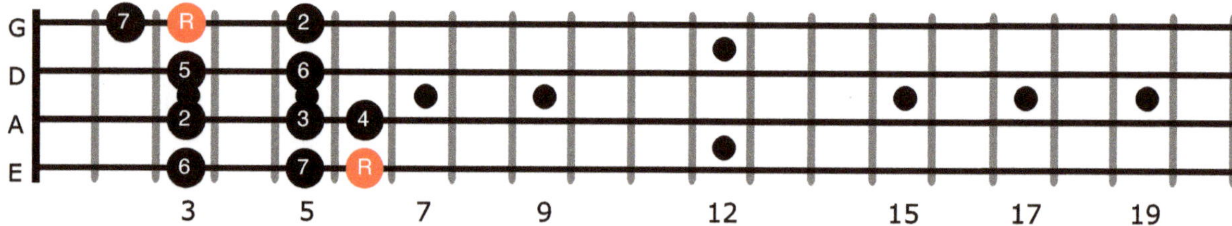

Gmi

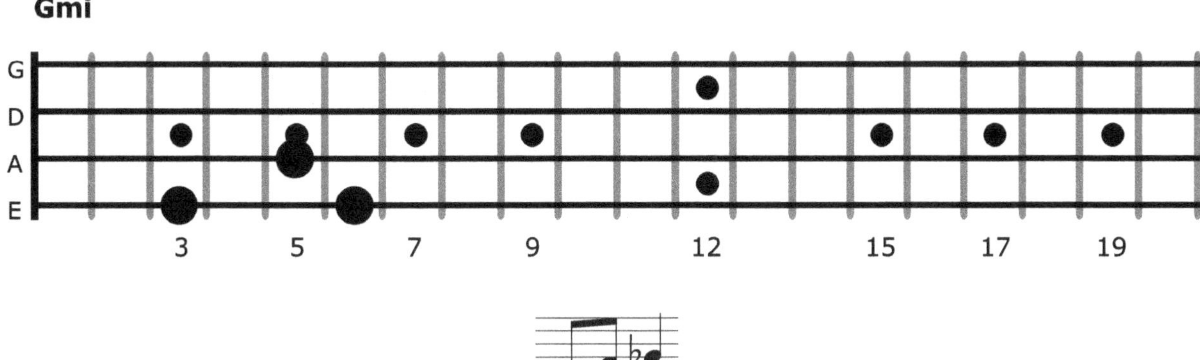

Adim

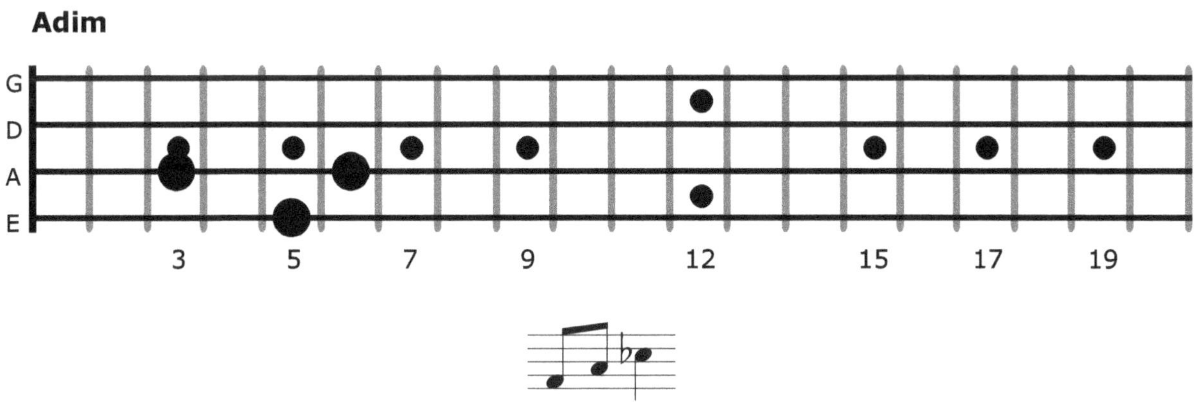

Bbma

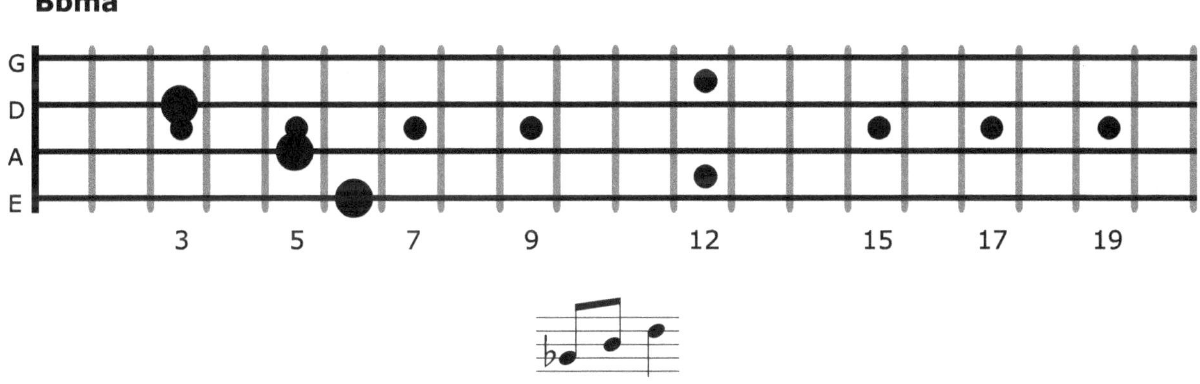

Cmi

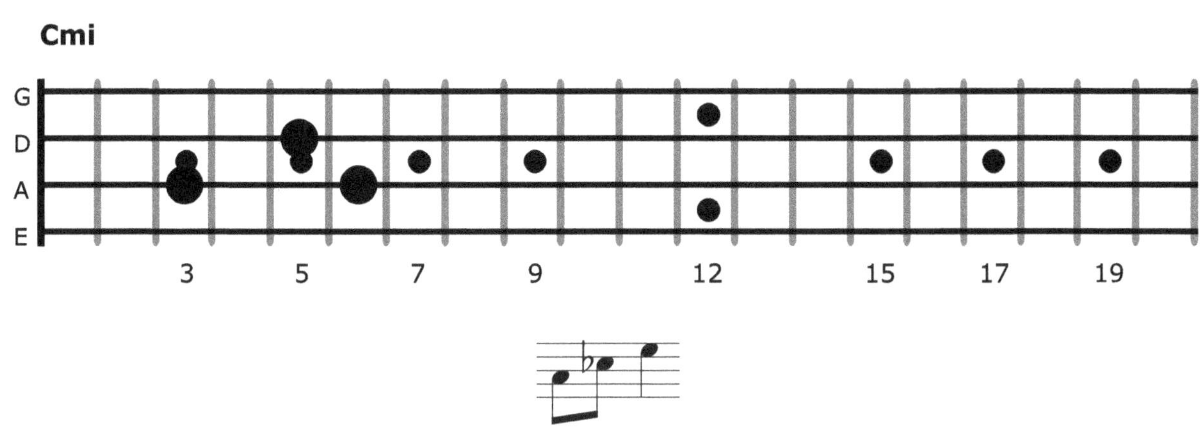

Dmi

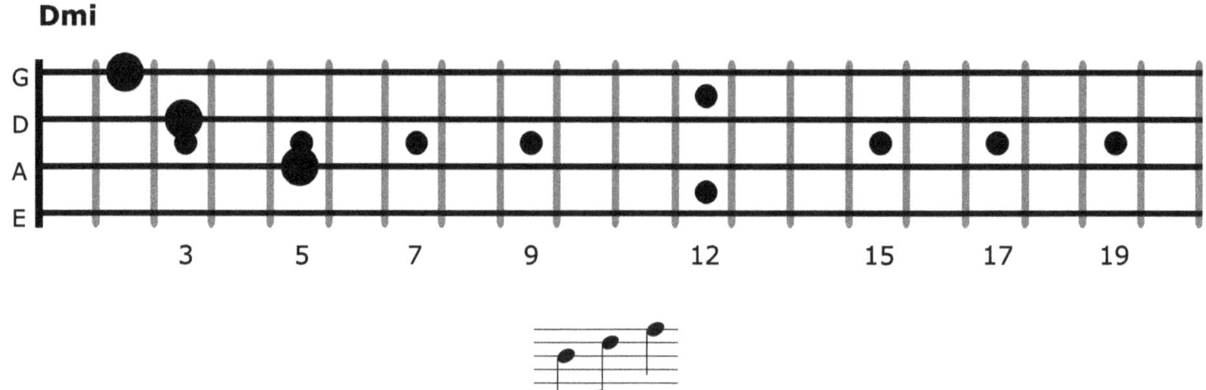

Ebma

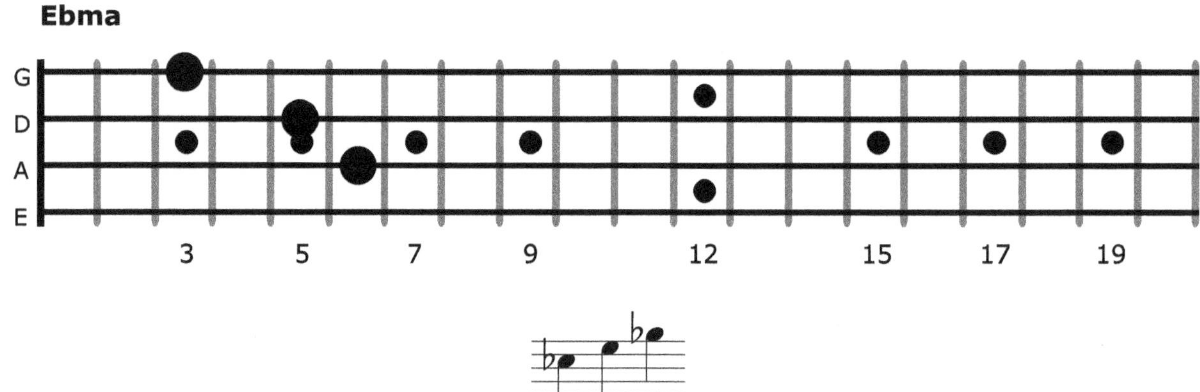

Fma

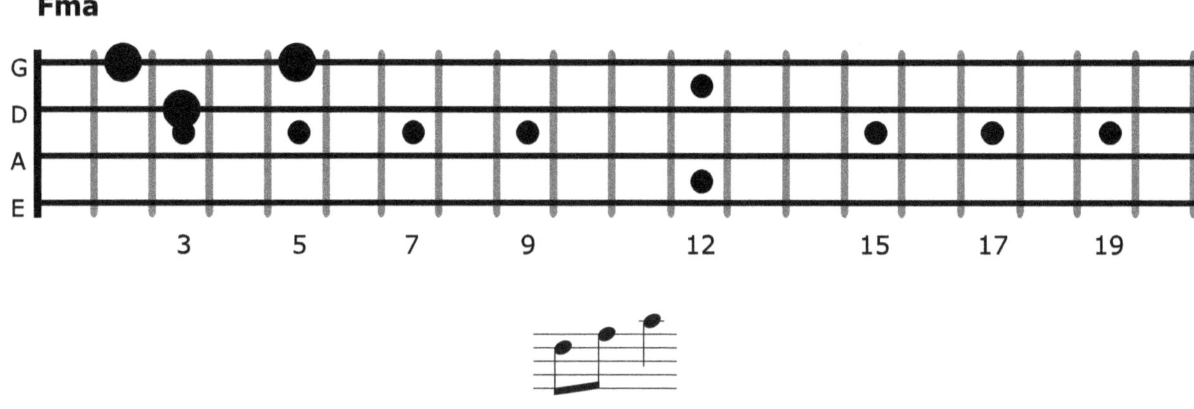

Play all of the triad arpeggios as one continuous exercise. Notice the resolution to the root of the key ("Bb"). This occurs at the top and bottom of the position. Remember that all of the notes should played where they are located in this position shape.

I have left the chord names off of the fretboard diagrams for the rest of the positions. I encourage you to identify the chords as you practice them. Remember that each position in this key will have the same seven diatonic triads. You will find, however, that some chords shapes (fingerings) will be different due to the position change.

The next position is located at the fifth fret "A/Bb". Continue to arpeggiate the diatonic triads of "Bb" in this position

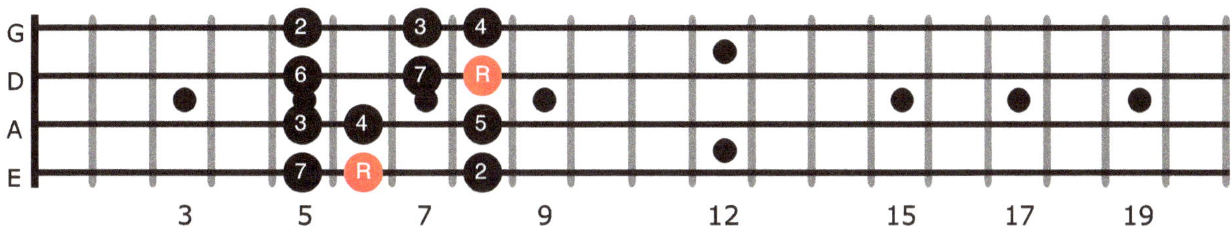

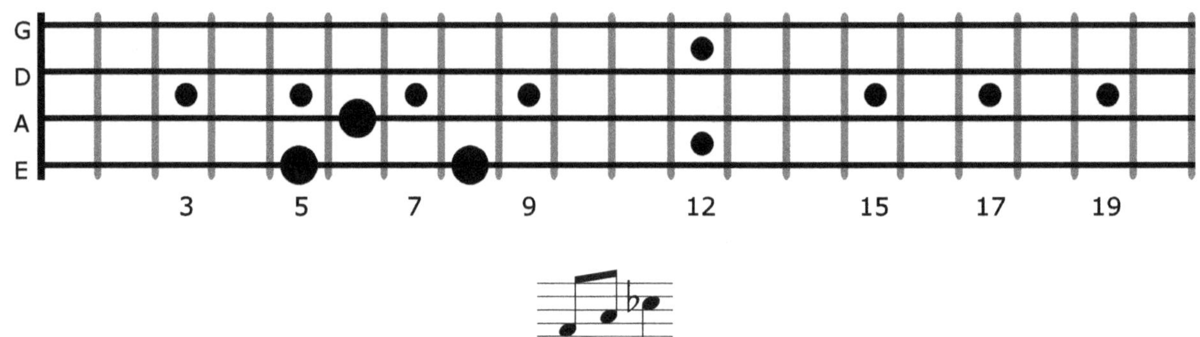

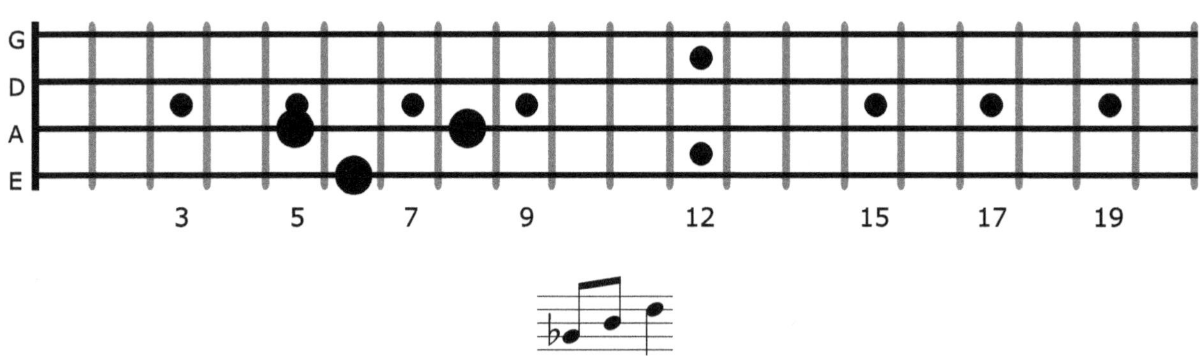

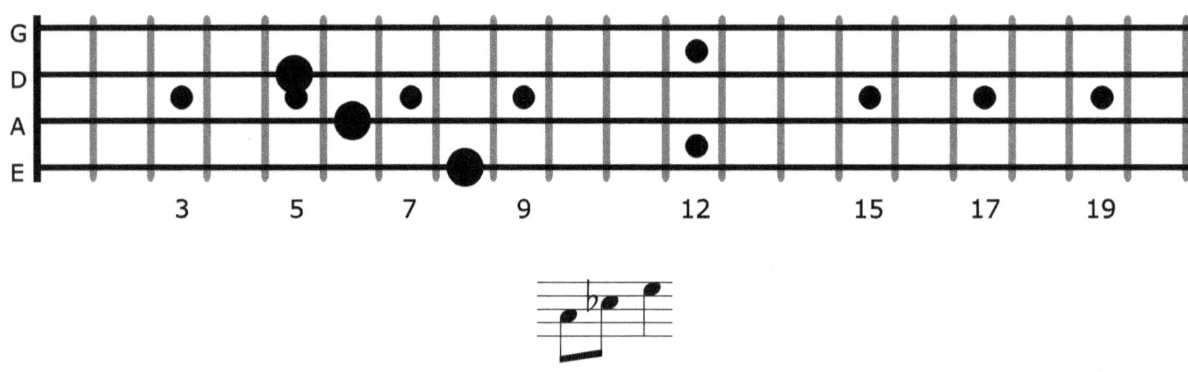

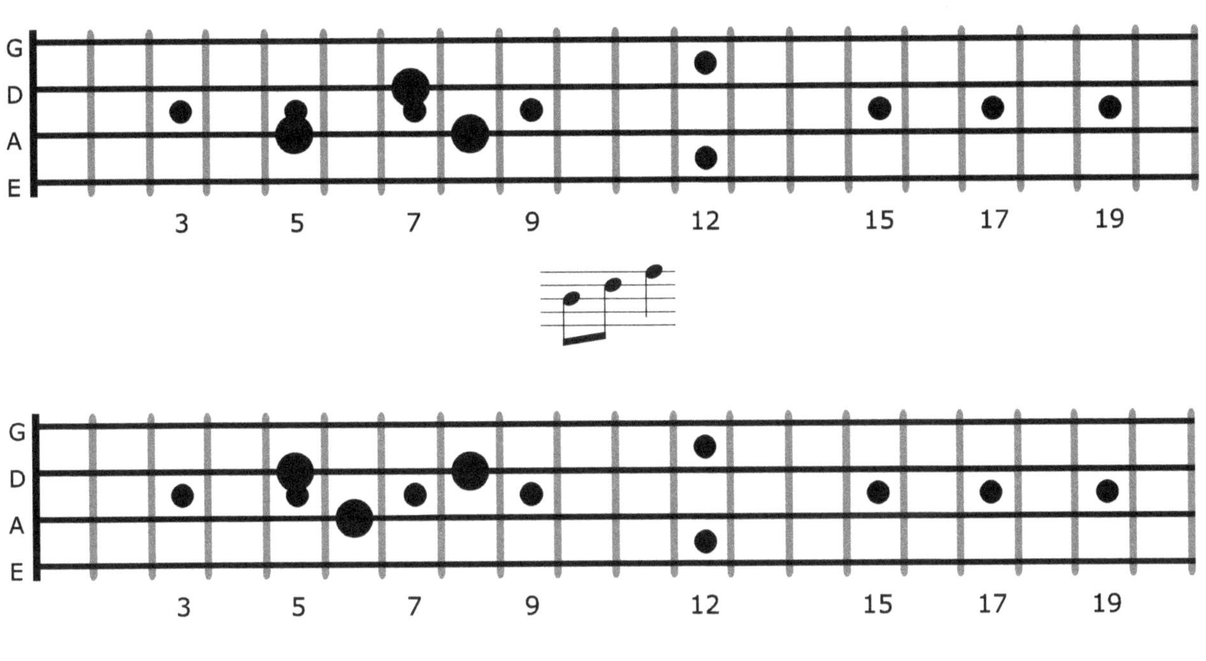

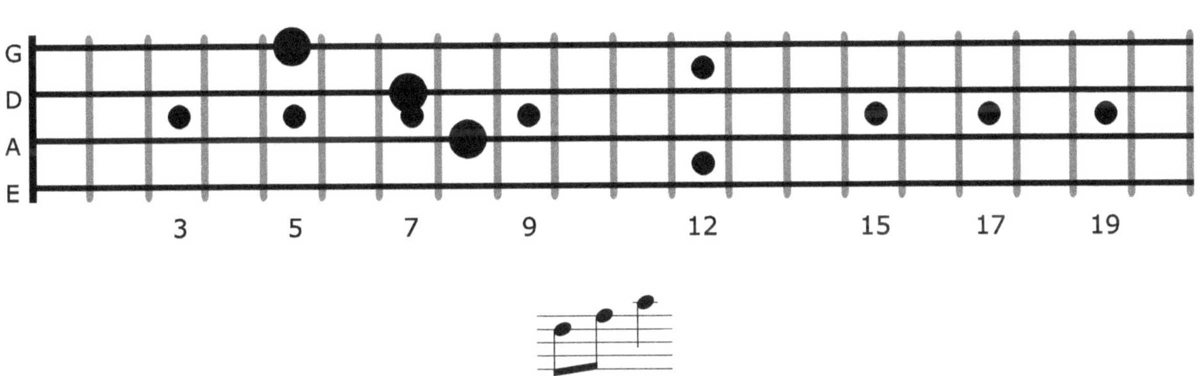

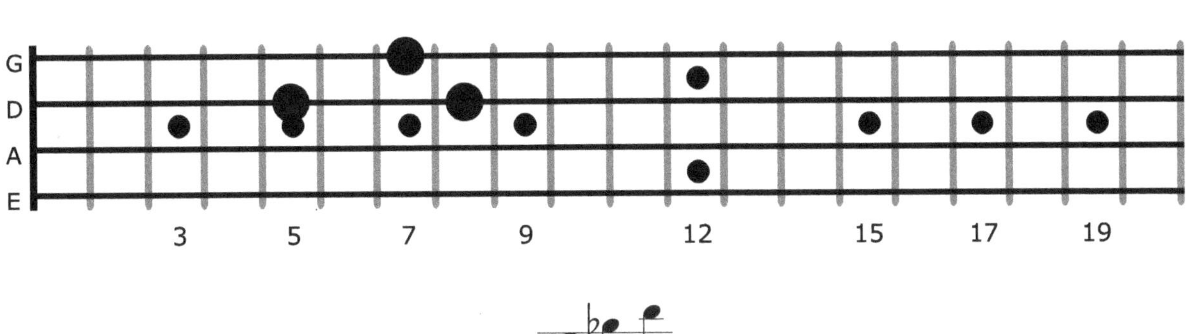

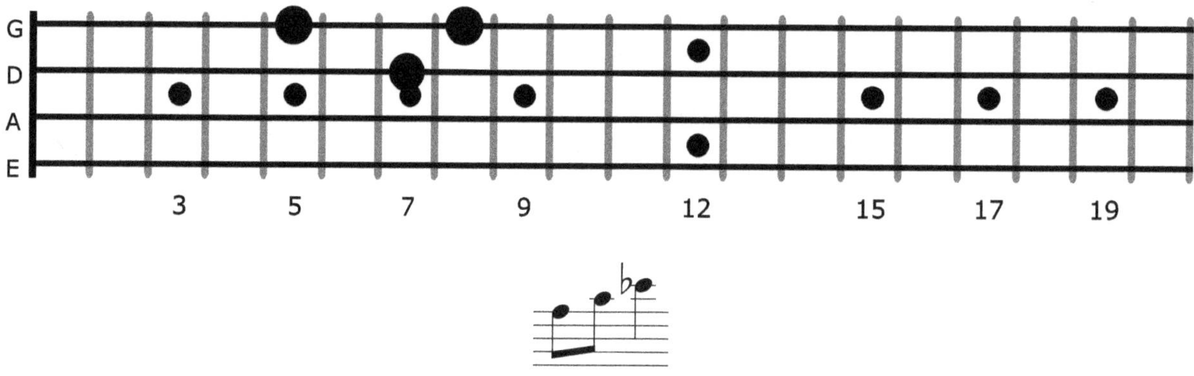

Play all of the triad arpeggios as one continuous exercise. Notice the resolution to the root of the key ("Bb"). This occurs at the top and bottom of the position. Remember that all of the notes should played where they are located in this position shape.

Play the triads of "Bb" in the position at the eighth fret. Cmi is the lowest arpeggio available in this position.

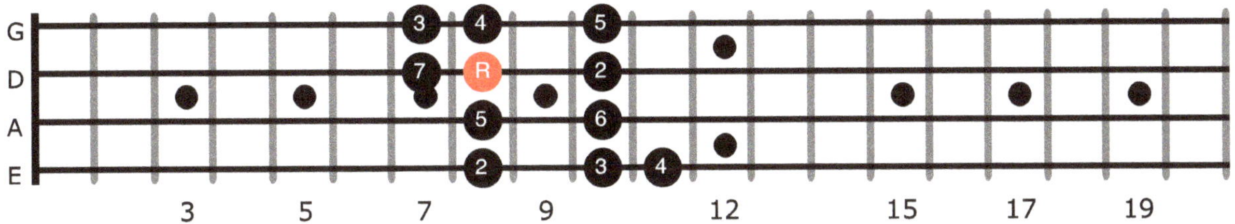

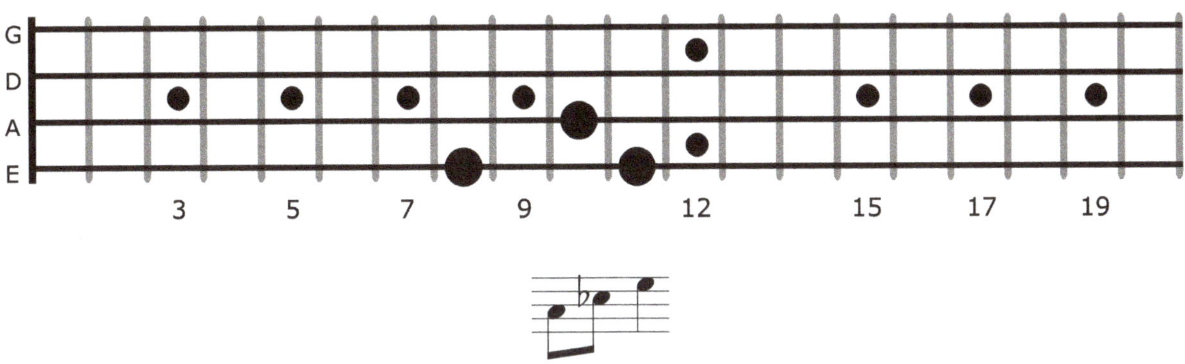

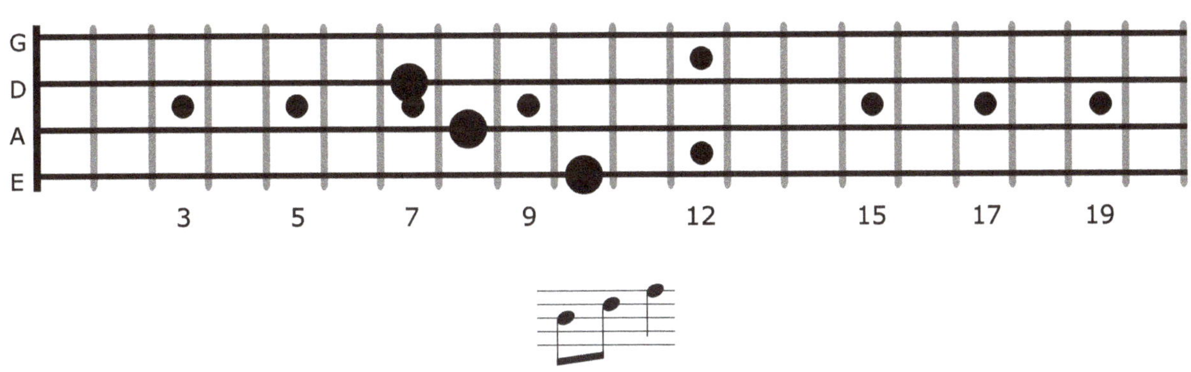

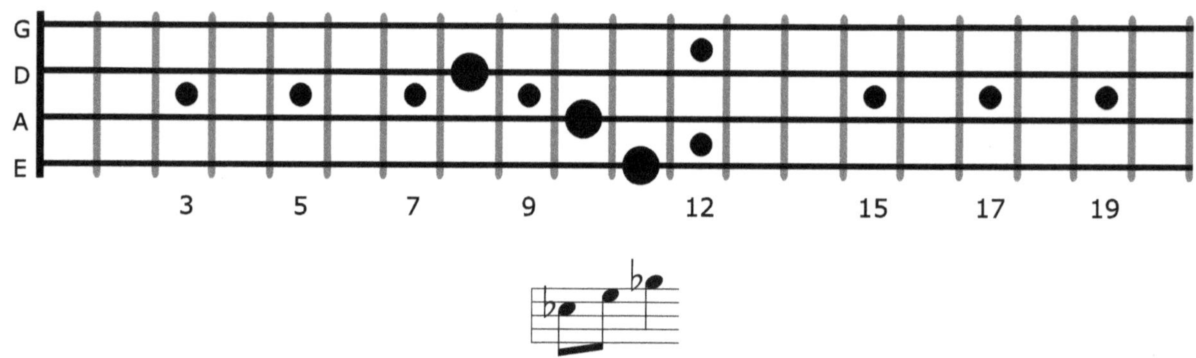

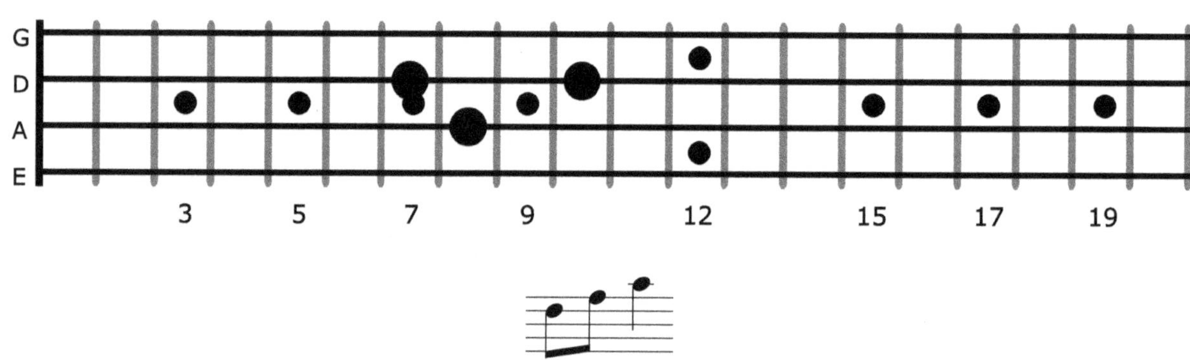

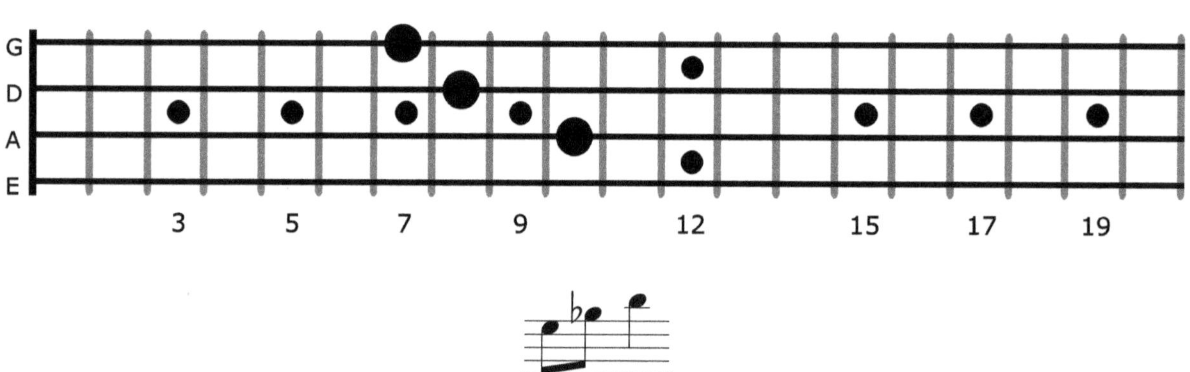

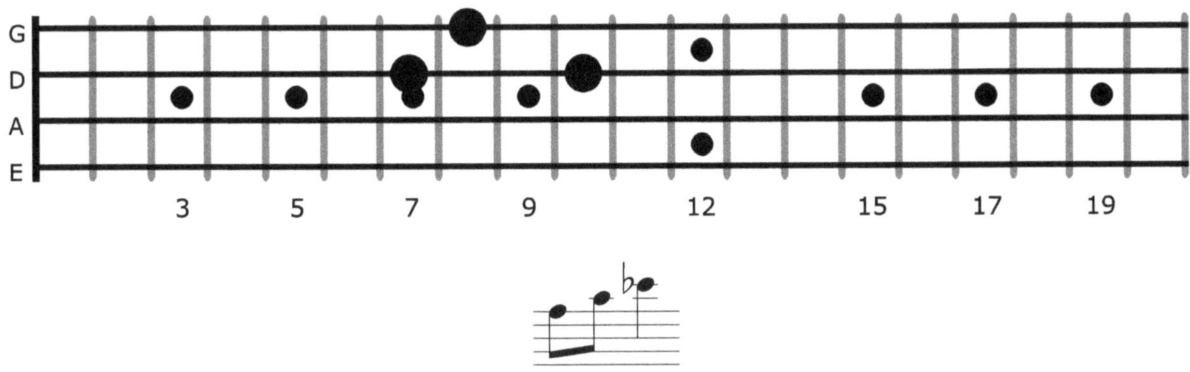

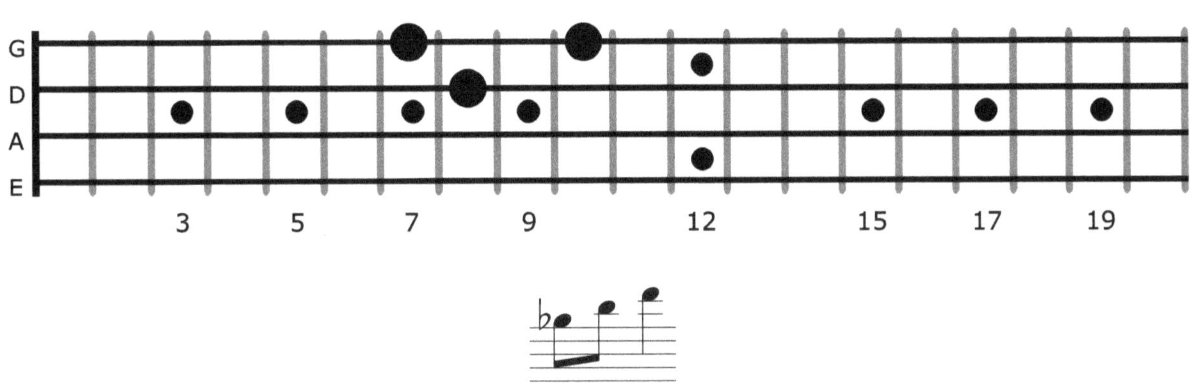

Play all of the triad arpeggios as one continuous exercise. Notice the resolution to the root of the key ("Bb"). This occurs at the top and bottom of the position. Remember that all of the notes should played where they are located in this position shape.

The next position is located at "D" at the tenth fret.

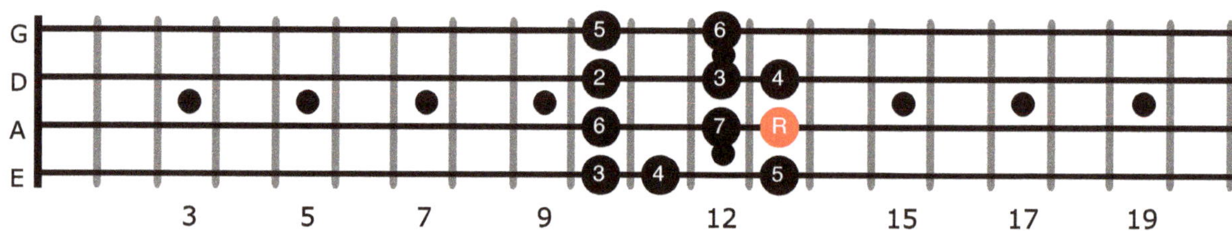

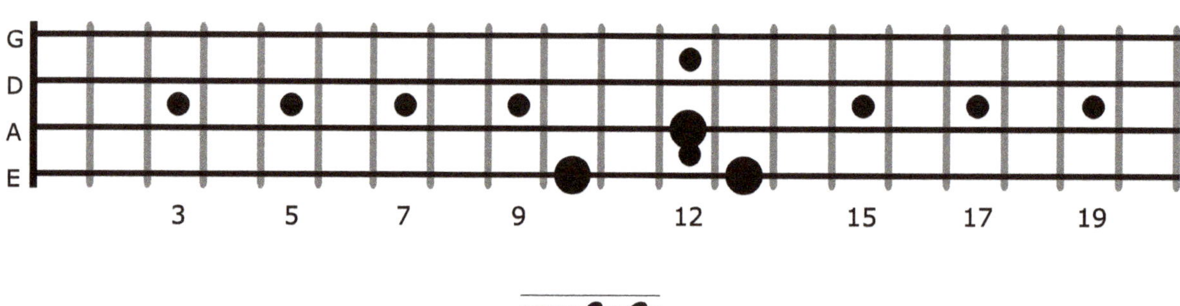

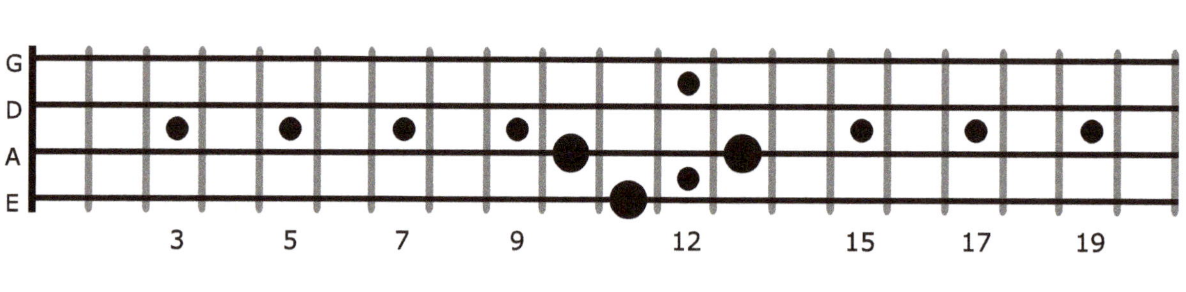

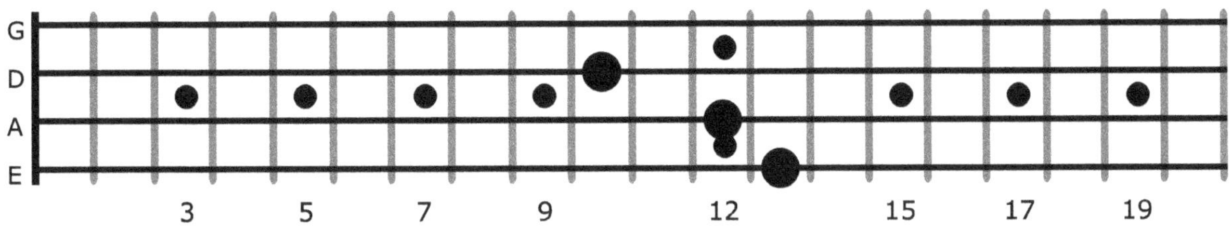

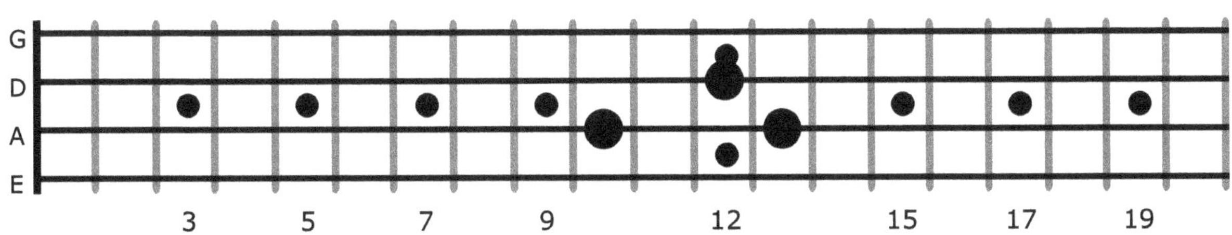

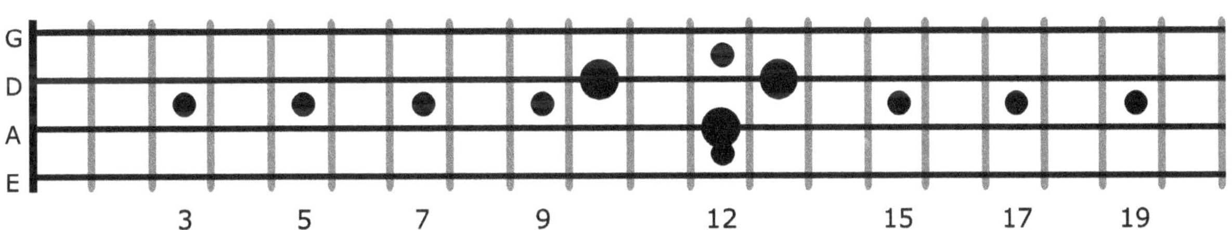

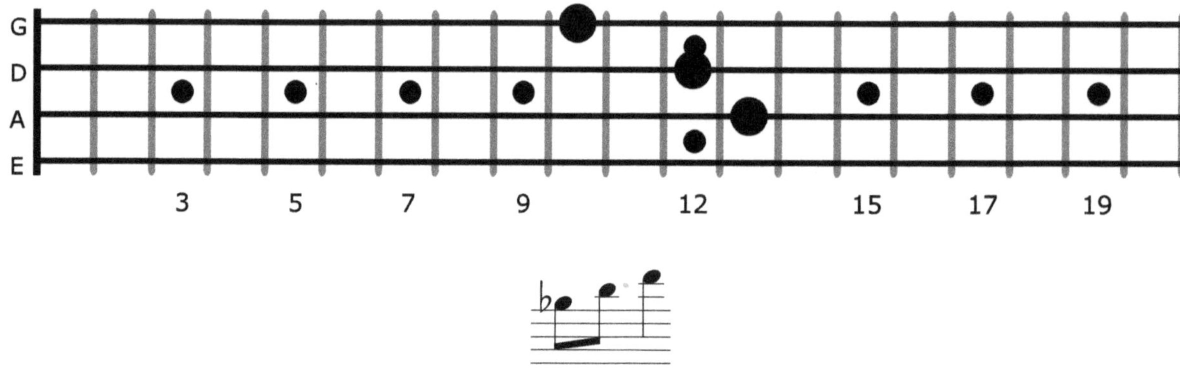

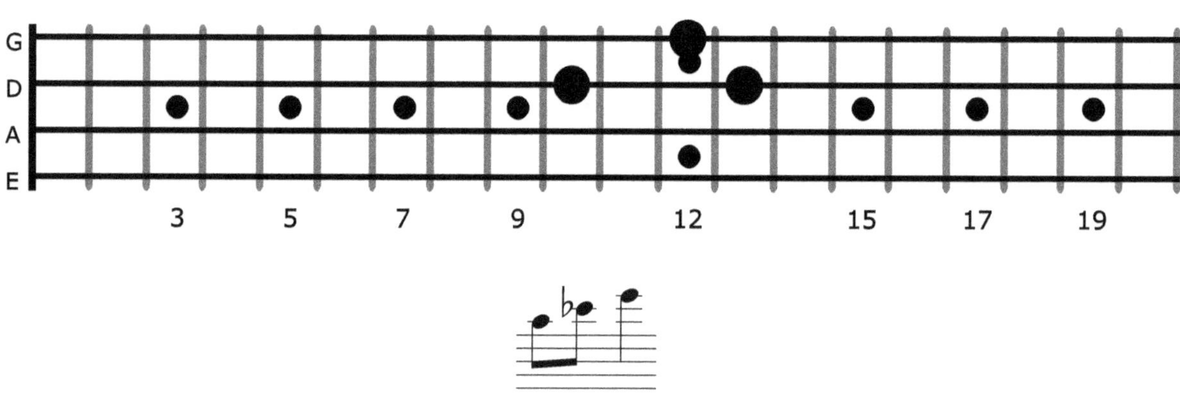

Now again, practice all of the triad arpeggios as one continuous exercise. Notice the resolution to the root of the key. Remember that all of the notes should played where they are located in this position shape.

The last position of the key of "Bb" is at the thirteenth fret starting on "F".

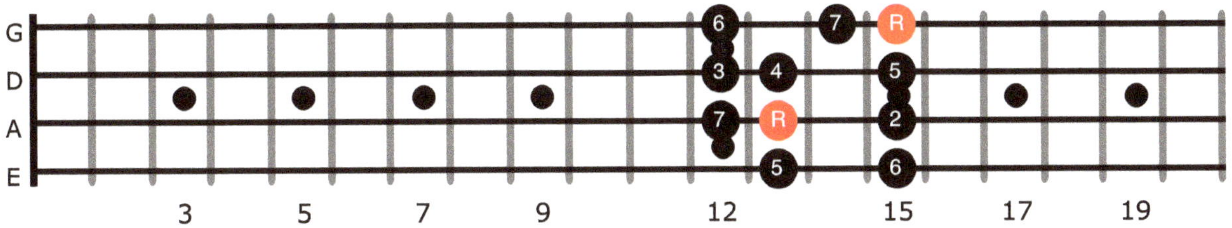

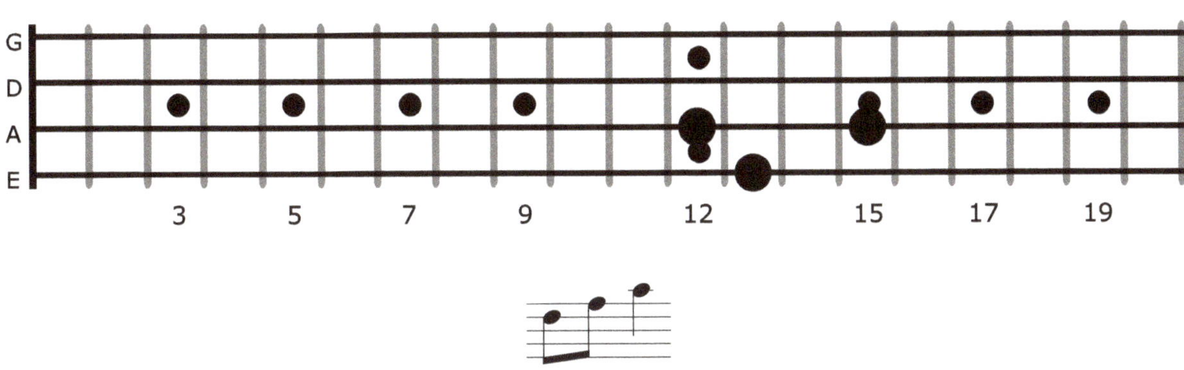

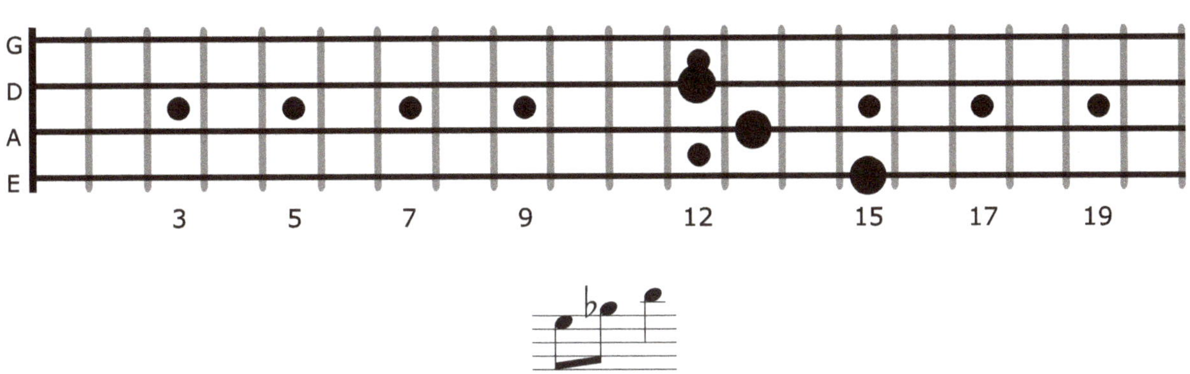

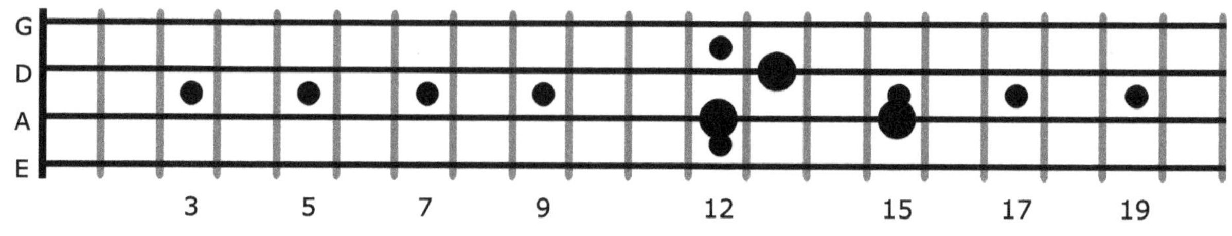

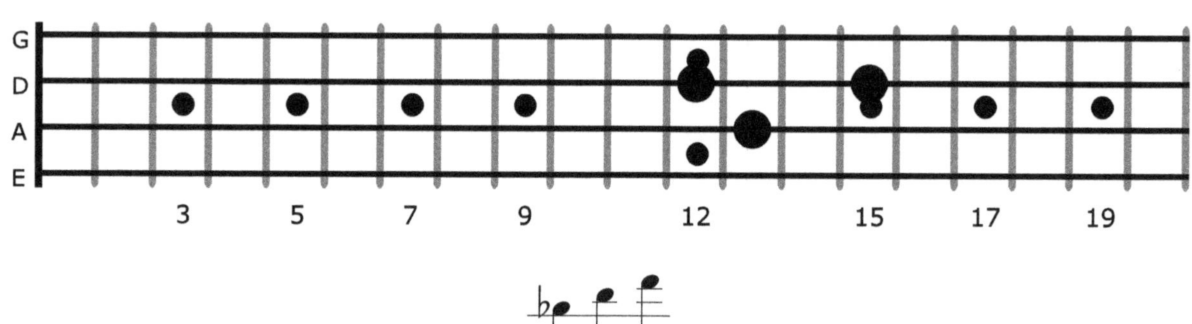

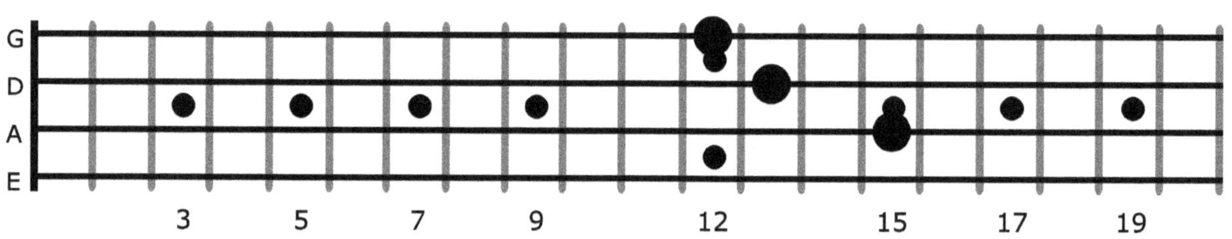

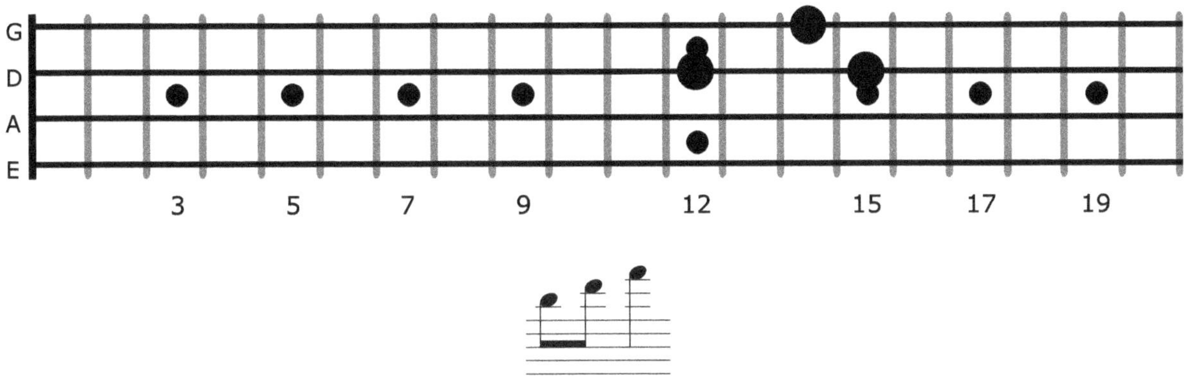

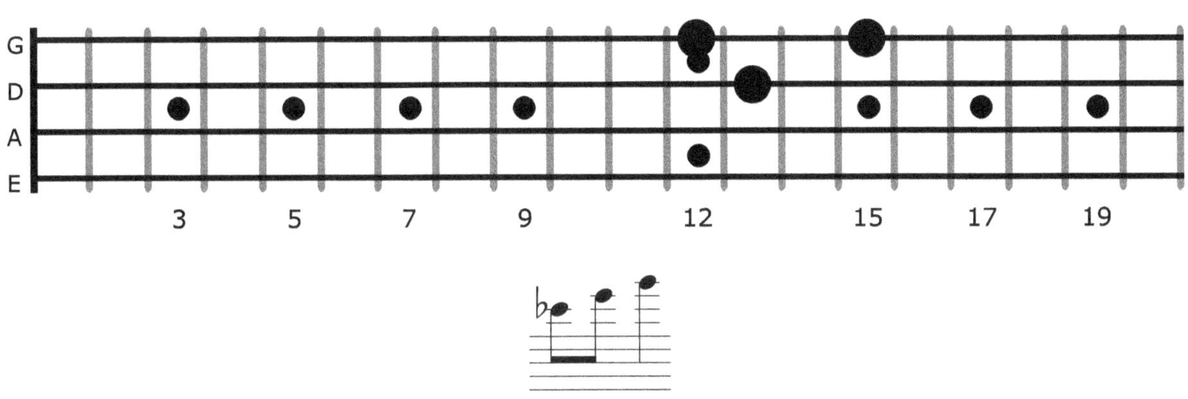

Practice all of the triad arpeggios as one continuous exercise. Notice the resolution to the root of the key. Remember that all of the notes should played where they are located in this position shape.

As was done for both the sequence and interval drills, the next step for the triad arpeggios is to move from a single position (**vertical**) approach to the **horizontal** approach. The five positions will be the map as we shift up and down the neck.

Starting each arpeggio from a single string will require shifting to a new position each time the interval of a whole step occurs between chord roots. When a half step separates chord roots (III-IV and VII-I), those sets of chords will be played in a single position.

E AND A STRING ARPEGGIOS

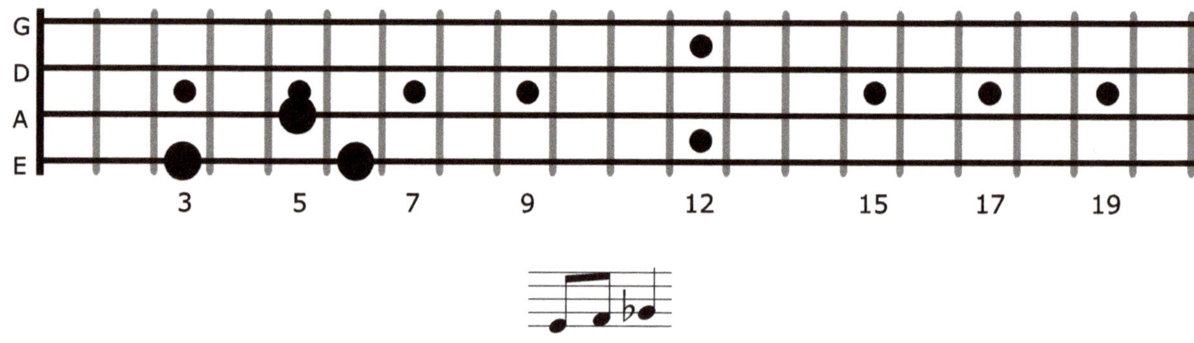

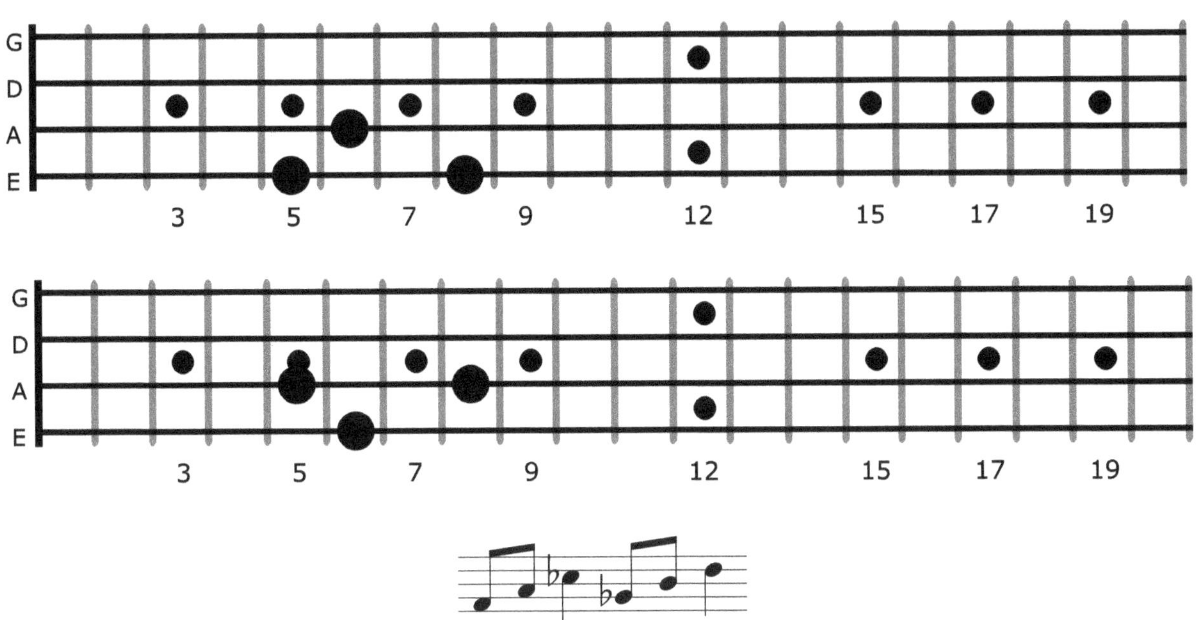

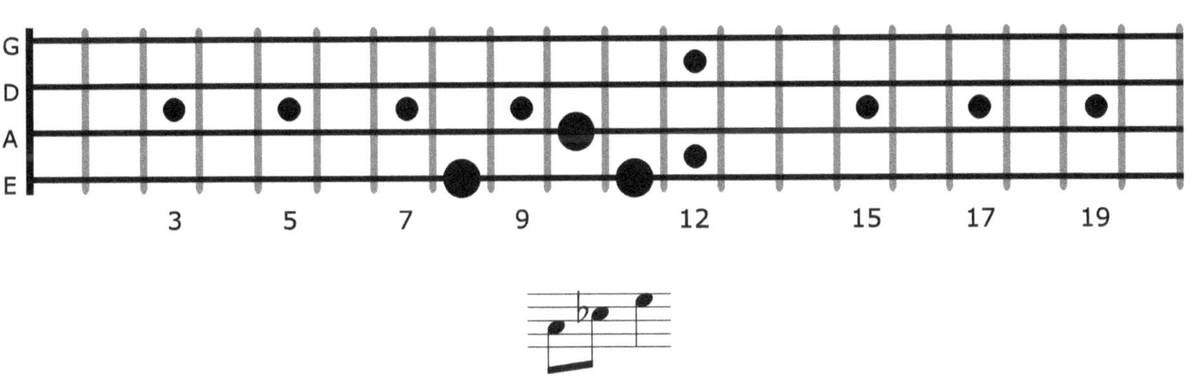

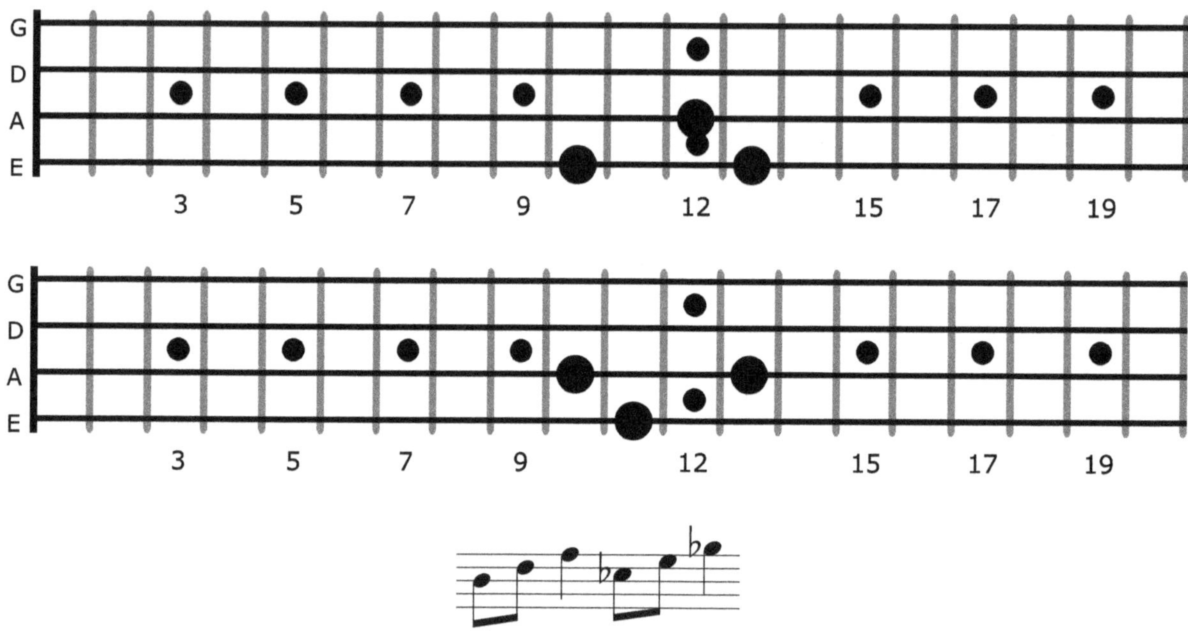

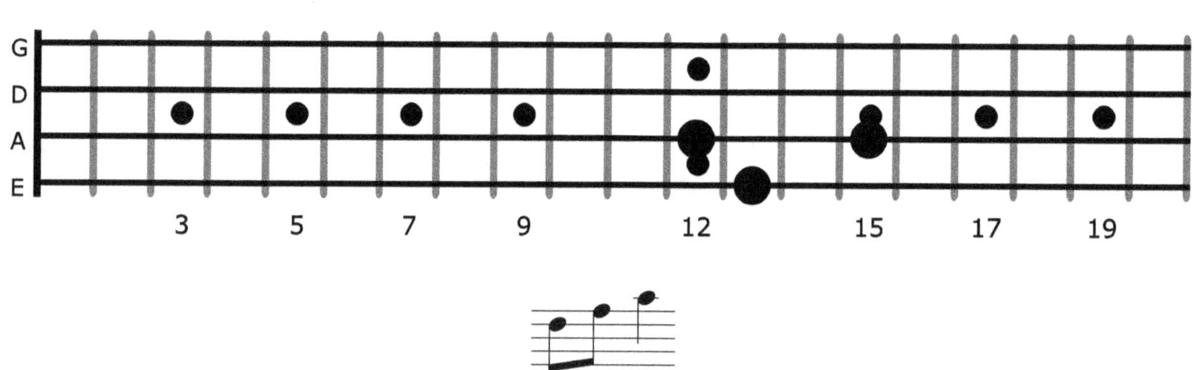

Now play all of the triads in a continuous exercise. Each triad will be played with roots on the E string only. The five positions will serve as a guide to create a logical shifting guide.

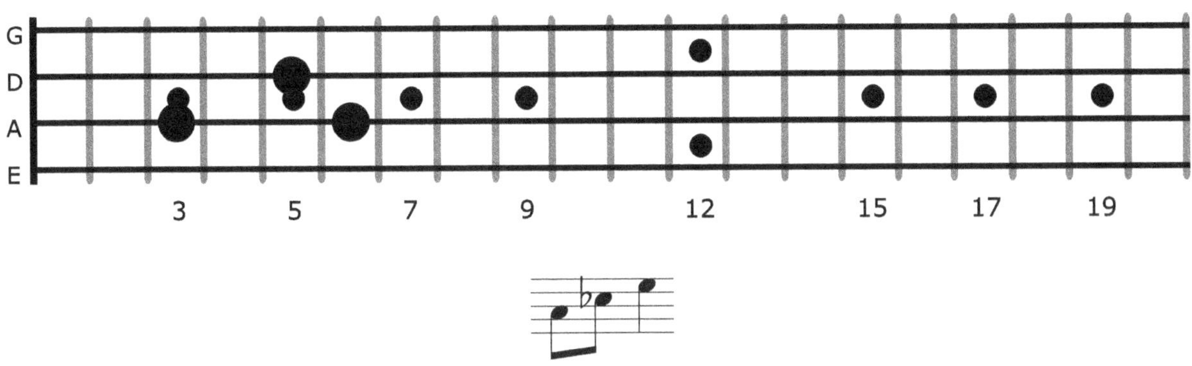

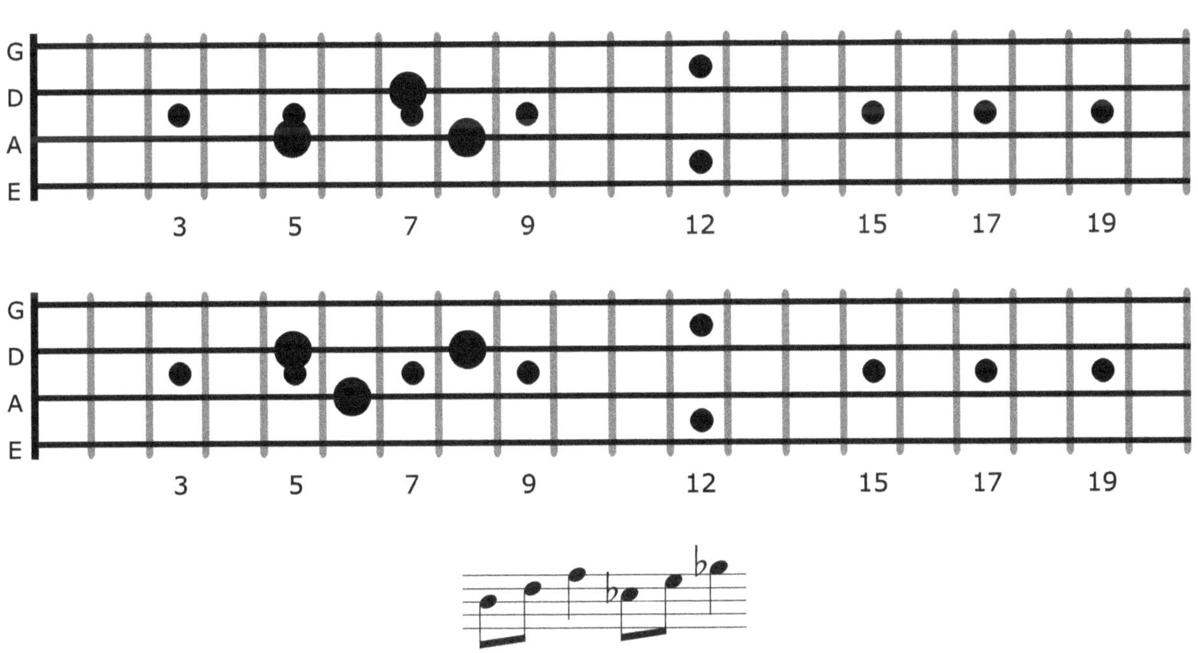

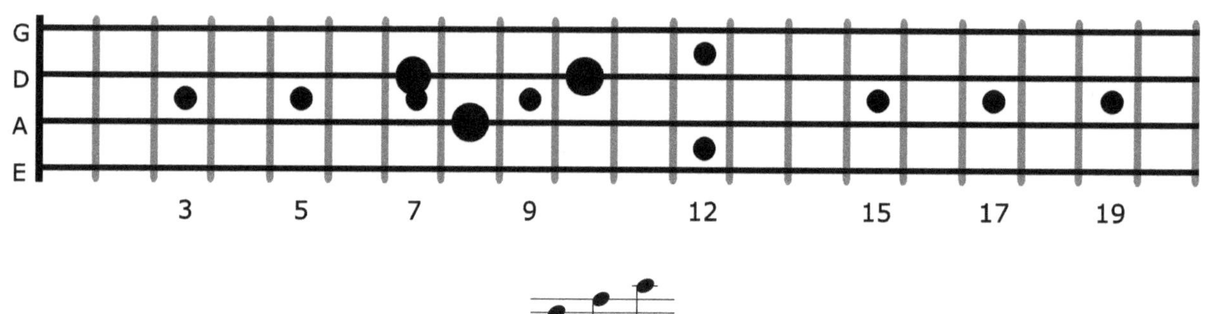

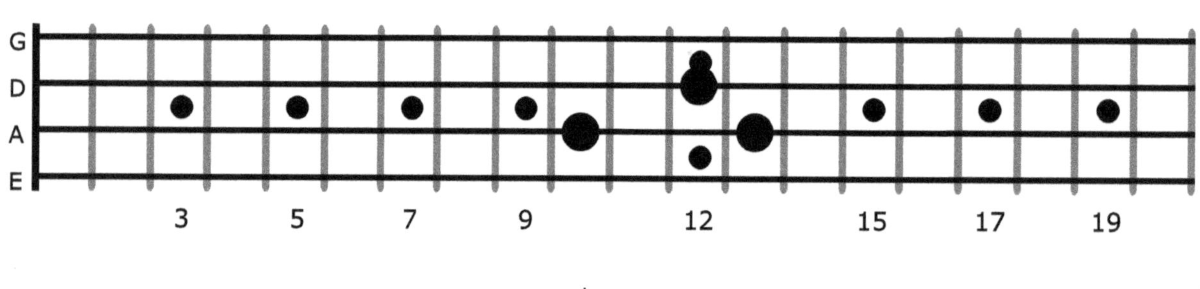

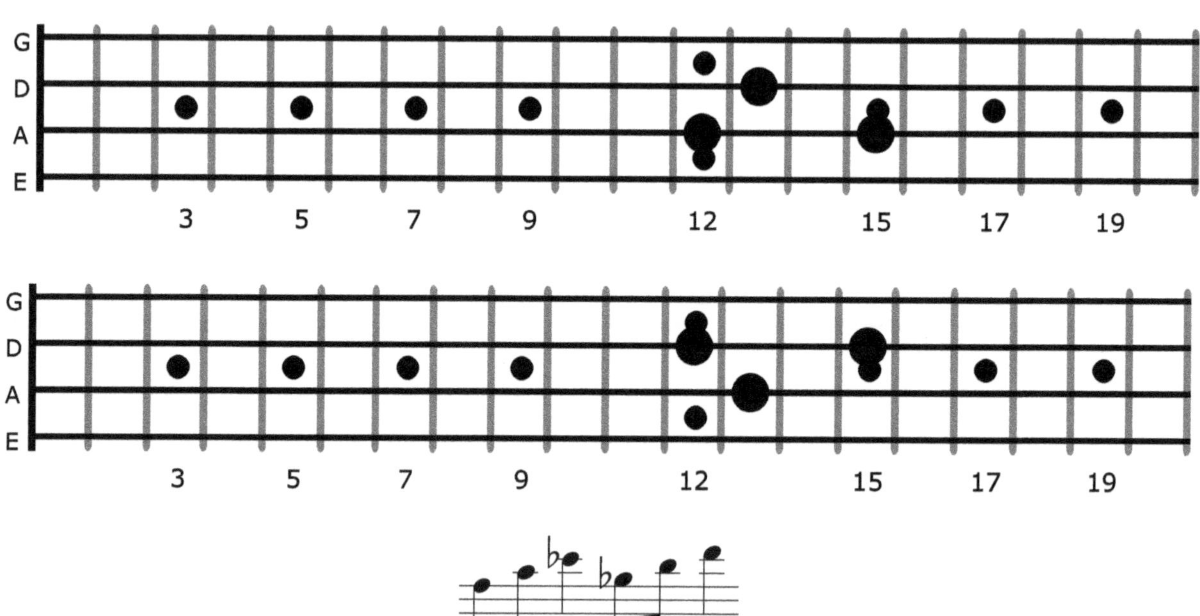

Play this continuous drill up and down *(horizontal)* the neck. Each triad will be played with roots on the A string only. The five positions will once again serve as the guide to establish a logical shifting strategy. Remember, roots a whole step apart ("C" to "D") will be arpeggiated in subsequent positions. Roots a half step apart ("D" to "Eb") will be played in the same position.

Last set of two string arpeggios is from the D string. The lowest triad from the key of "Bb" on the D string (remember no open strings) is Fma. Arpeggiate the triads on the D string.

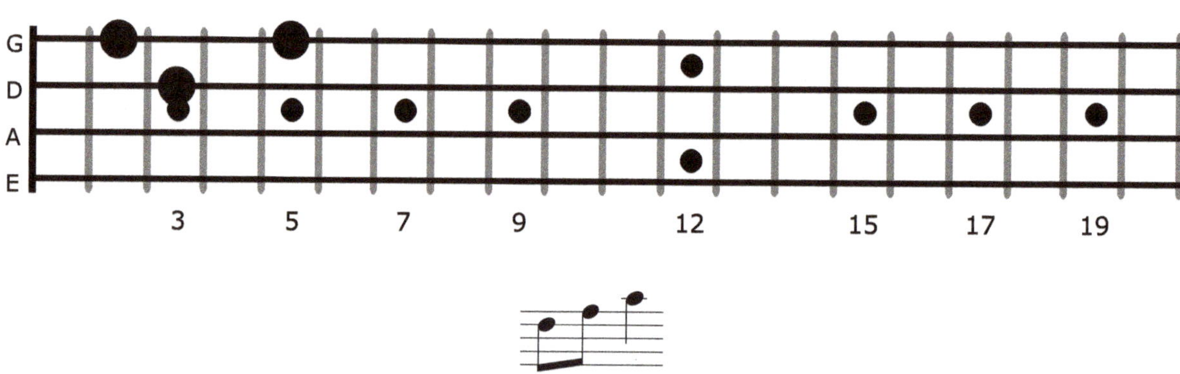

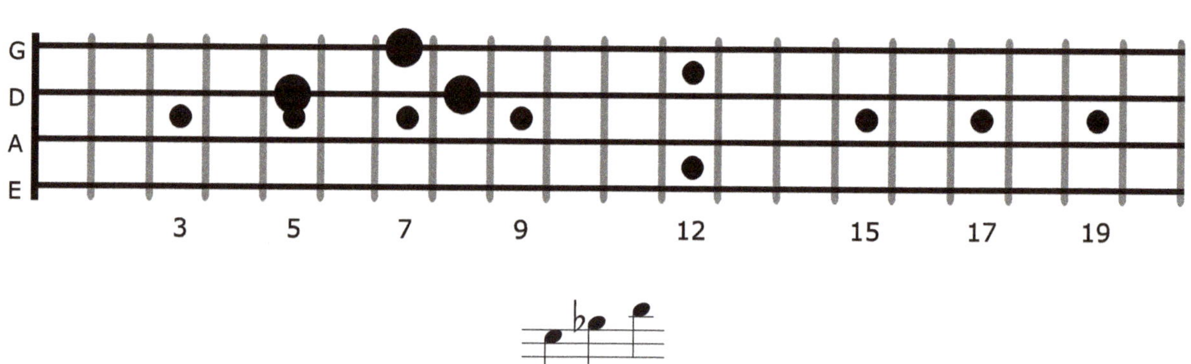

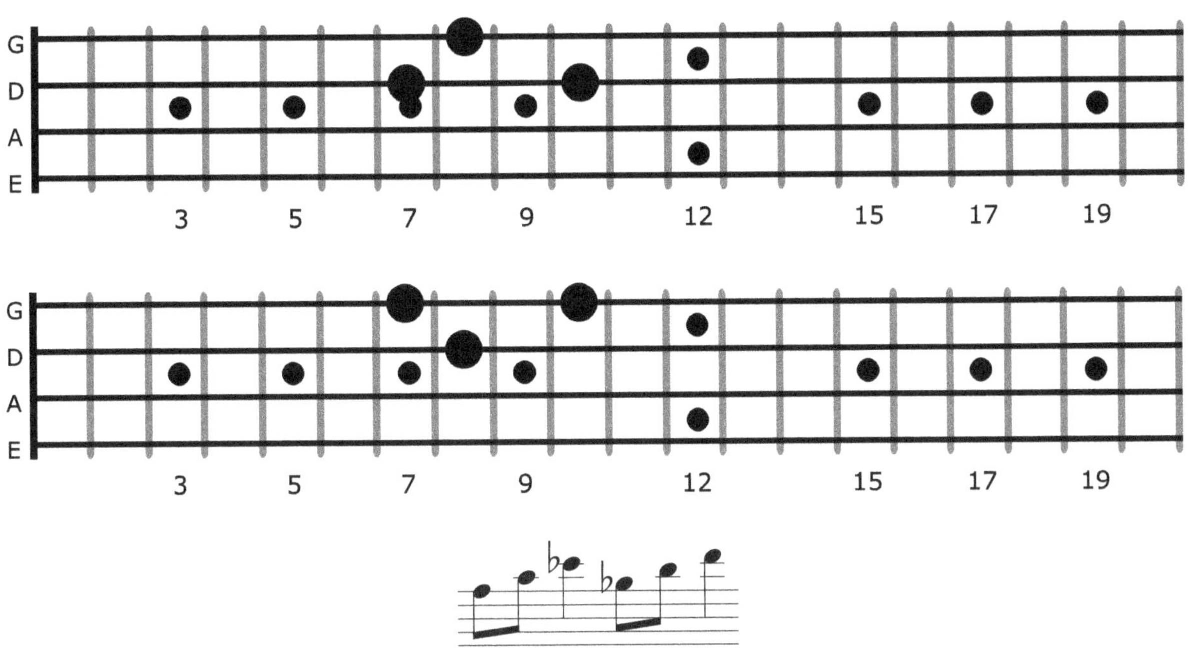

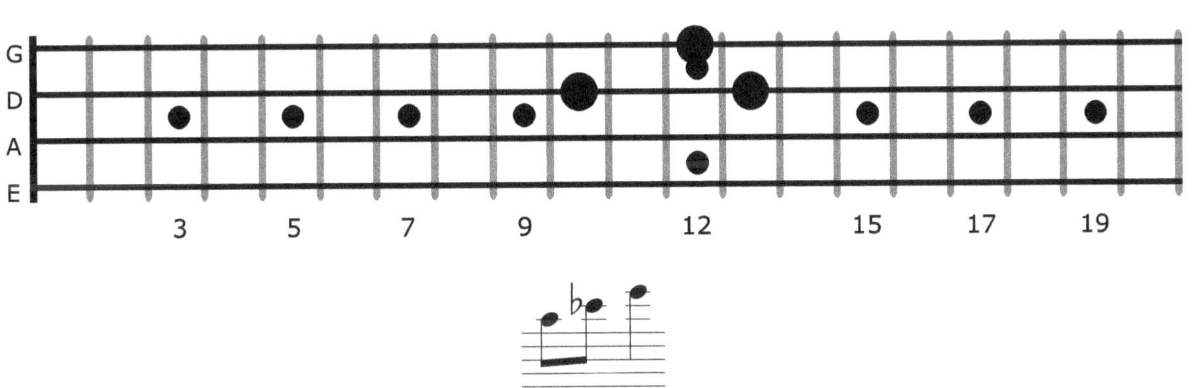

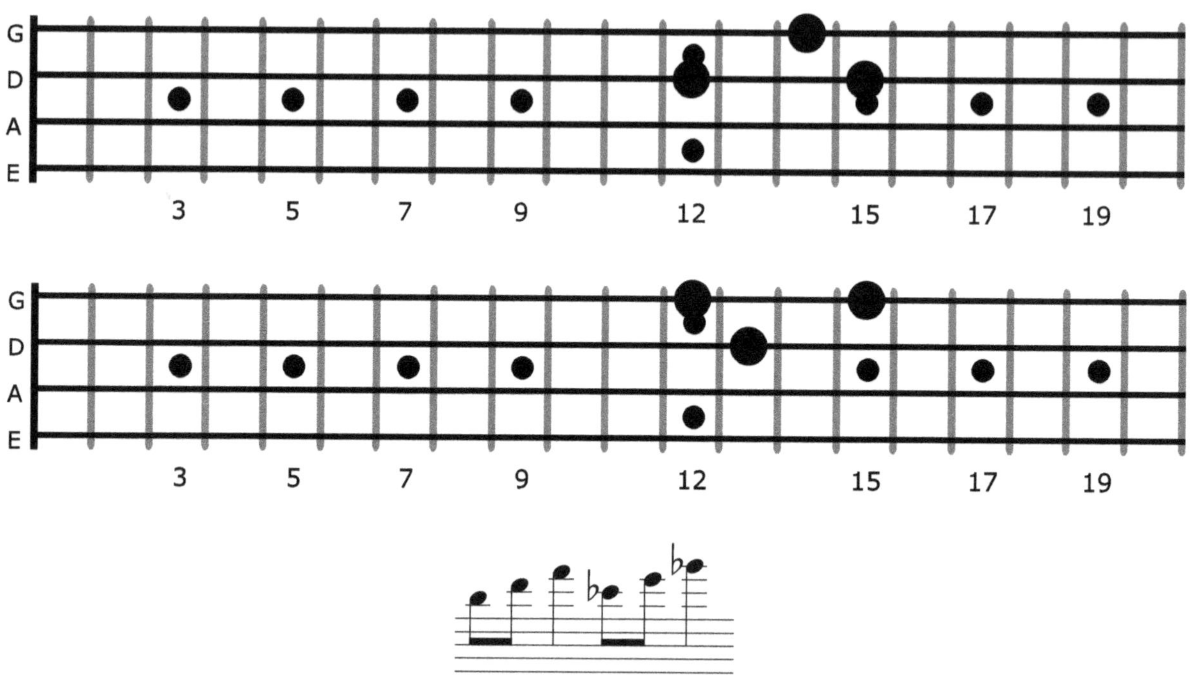

Play this continuous drill up and down *(horizontal)* the neck. Each triad will be played with roots on the D string only. The five positions will once again serve as the guide to establish systematic shifting.

Now play through these examples of bass lines constructed using triads from the key of "Bb" major.

This groove should be played in a single position located at the fifth fret ("A"/Bb"). The triads are Bbma, Ebma, Fma and Dmi.

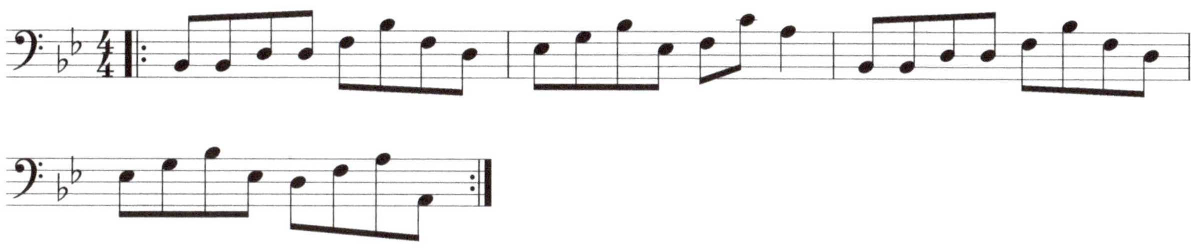

This groove requires several position shifts in order to play logically. The triads used for constructing this groove are Bbma, Ebma and Cmi and back to Bbma. Notice that the third is arranged above the fifth of the chord. In bass vernacular this is typically referred to as a "tenth" and is the third up an octave from the fundamental chord arpeggio. The quality of the tenth is identical to the third of the chord. Major tenth on major triads and minor tenth on minor triad. Play each chord root on the E string.

This last chapter will outline several advanced variations of the drills used in the book. One of the goals and tools of learning, is to develop an understanding of a challenge and to use it to create new challenges. In other words, re-arrange it to create new and often more challenging exercises. Variations of an exercise can often sound even more musical and create a sense of further control of the language. The vocabulary of music can be understood as numbers and thus re-arranged or sequenced in that way. Continue to play the new drills both *"vertically"* (inside a single position) and *"horizontally"* (shifting up and down the neck using the positions as a guide).

SEQUENCE

Take for instance the sequence drill from the second chapter. The drill was a four-note *ascending* sequence. Starting from each note of the key, (in a position and then two strings) the music "math" was 1234, 1234, 1234 repetitively.

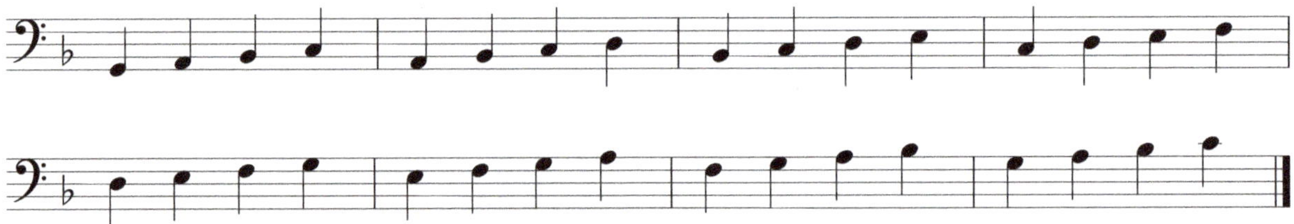

First, try *descending* the sequence 4321, 4321, 4321. You will still move the sequence up "alphabetically" (C Bb A G…D C Bb A…) through each position and then two strings approach.

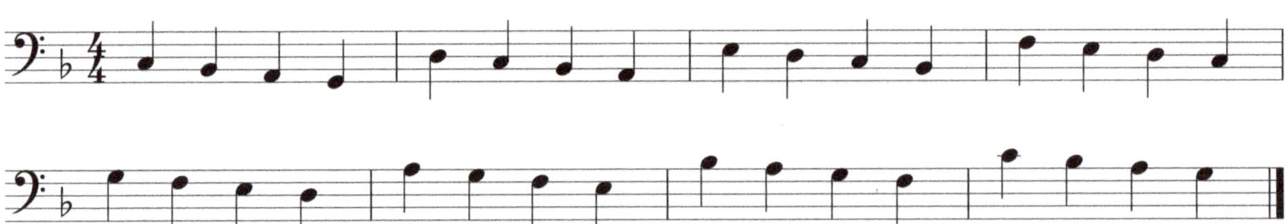

Next practice this sequence using the ***one up, one down*** sequence. This approach will alternate between an ascending and then descending sequence. 1234, 4321, 1234, 4321 repeatedly as you move through each position (vertical) or up and down the neck (horizontal).

There are numerous ways to vary this basic sequence, in addition to countless other sequences to be studied. To create your own (do it!) be organized (music "*math*") and disciplined (strict practice guidelines). <u>Do not use exceptions</u> to facilitate easy shortcuts for problems encountered. The organization and discipline will help you learn new vocabulary.

Using the variations outlined in the sequence drills, an identical approach should be practiced with the interval drills. In the initial exercise, the "root" of the interval (r-3, r-3, r-3, repeatedly) was played first, followed by the diatonic third above. This is an ***ascending*** approach. The interval of a third from each note in a position or up from a single string shifting up the neck.

However, we can reverse the drill to create a ***descending*** approach (3-r, 3-r, 3-r, repeatedly). Play this even as you move through each position, or up and down the neck.

And like the sequence drill, try alternating the interval exercise in a ***one up, one down*** pattern (r-3, 3-r, r-3, repeatedly)

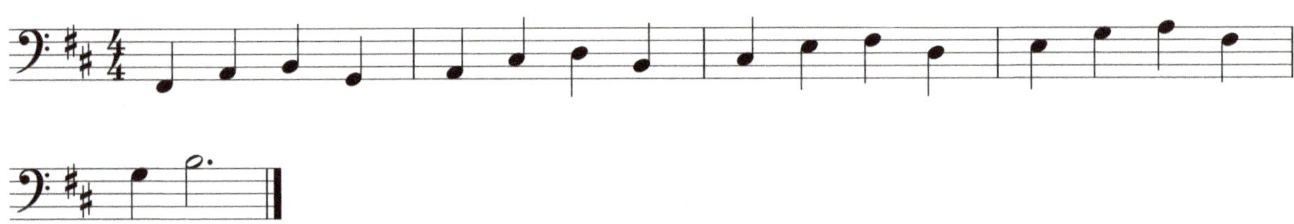

Using the same variations, play the diatonic triad arpeggios from the key of "Bb" major. The first drill was an *ascending* arpeggio.

Here is the *descending* arpeggios drill. Don't mistake these as inversions of a triad. The root of each triad is still the low voice (note).

And now the *one up, one down* version of the diatonic triads. Move this drill through each of the positions and up and down the neck, shifting through all positions.

Practice these bass lines and identify examples of vocabulary and variations derived from the exercises outlined throughout the book. In addition, try to identify the harmonic (chord) structure implied by the bass lines.

PRACTICE GROOVES

Play this in a single position ("B/C") at the seventh fret. In this groove the use of "*up one, down one*" arpeggios, sequences and interval examples are present.

PRACTICE GROOVES

In this example, shifting up the neck early (*second and fourth measures should be played in three different positions*) puts you in the best position to play the high "F#".

Start this bass line at "F" (eighth fret) on the A string. In measure three, play the arpeggios (Gmi, Ami and Bbma) by shifting back up the neck toward the position where the groove started.

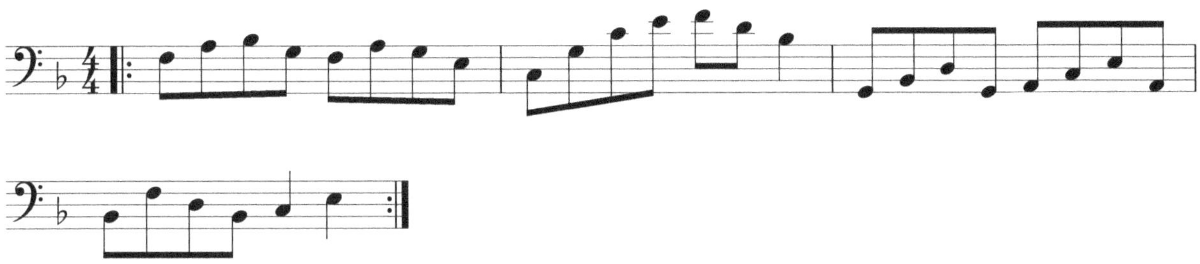

This groove in "D" major can be played is a single position at the fifth fret. In addition, try moving the sequence in the fourth measure down A and D strings starting at the ninth fret of the A string.

Remember: Be organized, use strict guidelines (so that you can duplicate exercises exactly in all keys) and practice using both a **vertical** (positions) and a **horizontal** (shifting up and down the neck) approach. The discipline gives us tools and methods to learn new vocabulary.

David Keif is a freelance bass player, living in Los Angeles, Ca. He maintains an active schedule of live performances and recording sessions. He also composes music for numerous tv shows and visual media of many types.

He has authored several instructional bass books that are published through Hal Leonard that are available online and in music stores globally.

For over thirty years, he has been on the teaching staff of **Musicians Institute** in Hollywood, Ca.